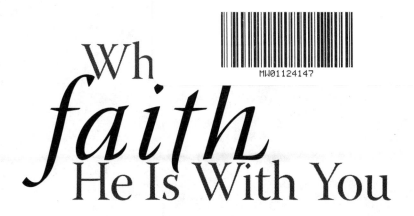

When faith He Is With You

One Woman's Journey of Faith and Her Husband's Battle with ALS

Viki Scherer

Where There Is

faith

He Is With You

One Woman's Journey of Faith and Her Husband's Battle with ALS

Viki Scherer

House of Prayer Ministries, Inc.
2428 W. Florian Court
Decatur, IL 62526

First Printing, June 2011

Where There Is Faith He Is With You Copyright © 2011 by Viki Scherer

Library of Congress Control Number: 2011905594

Published by

House of Prayer Ministries, Inc.
2428 W. Florian Court
Decatur, IL 62526
217-428-7077
www.houseofprayerminstries.com

Printed in the United States of America

ISBN 978-1-882825-23-3

Contents

Dedication and Acknowledgments

I am so grateful for God's grace, mercy, strength and faithfulness throughout my life's journey of faith and Doug's battle with ALS. I dedicate this book to our wonderful children, Michael and Sarah, who are gifts from God. May this testimony be a legacy of the love and commitment your dad and I had during our 27 years of marriage. To Michael's wife, Quinishai, I welcome you into our family!

I also dedicate this book to all the families who are struggling with ALS or any debilitating disease. You are not alone!

A big thank you goes to family members, friends, my "gas angel," neighbors, mass transit employees, teachers, union laborers, doctors, nurses, medical supply companies, my church Harvest Christian Center, other churches, the ALS Association St. Louis Regional Chapter, the Muscular Dystrophy Association, Washington University School of Medicine in St. Louis and Springfield, Illinois' Memorial Home Services Hospice. Your prayers, encouragement and unselfish expressions of love and financial blessings in our time of need were very much appreciated.

In particular I thank my mom, Dottie Henneberry, and my siblings and their spouses for the many times they assisted us: Kim and Cathie Henneberry, Chris Henneberry, Kirk and Jeanette Henneberry, and Cheri and Greg Bassana. Doug's family was a great source of encouragement, and I graciously thank them for all of their help. Thanks to my special friends Mark and Evvy Bowman, Craig and Kathy Patient, and Kathy Davis for their support before and after Doug's homecoming.

God works in mysterious ways and if it had not been for the ALS disease, Doug and I would have never met Robert and Andrea Floyd. We had a profound influence on their lives for all eternity, and I believe there are many others like them who will be touched in a powerful way because of our story.

Lastly, I want to thank those who were involved with the publication of this book including Sara Goodner, who read the manuscript, and Connie Peters for her encouraging support. In addition thanks goes to graphic artists Janet Barding, Katrina Fisher and Tammy Ward who work for my sister Cheri and her husband Greg's business Before U Print, Inc. The book looks great! Thanks, Cheri and staff, for all your wonderful assistance!

To God be the glory, for the things He has done!

Shalom!
Viki Scherer

Preface

If you are enduring a terrible disease, providing assistance as a caregiver, experiencing the loss of a loved one, or just struggling in your faith, I can identify and my heart goes out to you! *Where There Is Faith He Is With You* is a powerful testimony of God's faithfulness during a difficult time when my wonderful husband, Doug Scherer, was diagnosed with ALS, Lou Gehrig's Disease. It is a love story and commitment to our wedding vows "in sickness and in health."

There are many wonderful stories of God's miraculous provisions and numerous random acts of kindness. I must admit it was sometimes difficult being a recipient when we had always been givers. Proverbs 3:27 states, *"Do not withhold good from those who deserve it, when it is in your power to act."* My hope is that this book will encourage you to assist others when they are in need.

We had a national spotlight with the ALS disease and were blessed with opportunities to share our faith in Jesus Christ. By God's grace He used a horrible disease to touch the lives of others and allowed a wonderful glimpse into heaven.

I do not know why bad things happen to good people, but I can testify that God is with us, and He has a plan for our lives. *"'For I know the plans I have for you,' declares the Lord, 'plans to prosper you and not to harm you, plans to give you hope and a future'" (Jeremiah 29:11).* My prayer is that this book will be a source of encouragement no matter what you are going through and lead many individuals to the saving knowledge and truth of Jesus Christ as their Savior and Lord. *"For our light and momentary troubles are achieving for us an eternal glory that far outweighs them all" (II Corinthians 4:17).*

Viki Scherer

Chapter One

Luke 1:45 (NAMS) *"Blessed is she who believed that there would be a fulfillment of what had been spoken to her by the Lord."*

For six years the verse Luke 1:45 was my guiding force and source of hope and inspiration as I waited for my "knight in shining armor" to come back and ask me to be his bride. Douglas F. Scherer, better known as Doug, proposed to me the first time on a snowy, cold night in late January 1976 at Morton Park in Charleston, Illinois. His original intentions were to propose to me on Valentine's Day, but he could not wait that long. He was in love with me!

I was a senior at Eastern Illinois University, double majoring in journalism and speech communications. Doug had graduated five years earlier from Eastern with a music education degree. He was long gone from the school before I started and definitely would not have been my choice as a mate. He became a bona fide, long-haired "hippy" after graduation and hitchhiked to California twice, searching for the meaning of life. Although he decided not to go into teaching, he continued playing his trumpet. Later in life he discovered the value of his trumpet skills.

We met at an evening church service in October 1975 at the House of Prayer in Decatur, Illinois. I was a "women's libber" in my "B.C." days (before Christ) and vowed I would never get married, let alone have children. Throughout college I was career-oriented with the goal of eventually working for a major magazine. I worked part-time for one of my speech professors who was forever lecturing me that "smart" people needed to get married and have children so they could help run the world. That advice did not appeal to me. I grew up the oldest of five children and was second mother to them. The responsibility of taking care of my siblings helped me formulate the philosophy that a husband and children would just get in the way. Instead, I wanted freedom and a career. I wanted to see the world!

I even informed Doug shortly after I met him that I never wanted to get married. That had to be a bombshell for him because he had already determined I was the one for him. It was really bizarre how we even met in the first place.

My parents, Jerry and Dottie Henneberry, started the House of Prayer Ministries, Inc. in January of 1975. On August 11 of that year the ministry purchased the England mansion and "converted" it into the House of Prayer. Considered Decatur's most handsome home in 1916, this enormous house had 29 rooms and 10 bathrooms.

My mom was the first person to get saved in our family of seven. For a number of years she had been involved in the occult. A psychic woman, who was friends with my parents, gave my mom a copy of Hal Lindsay's book *The Late Great Planet Earth*. She found it to be interesting and thought my mom might enjoy it. Heavy conviction came upon my mom as she read the book and realized for the first time in her life that she was a sinner and needed to repent of her involvement in the occult. With no one around, she got down on her knees in our living room and prayed to accept Jesus Christ as her Savior. The date was June 25, 1973, her 39th birthday.

We knew something was different when she started reading the Bible out loud to us. Within a few months all five of us kids prayed to accept Christ as our Savior. Our dad, however, was skeptical and did not want to have anything to do with being born again. That just made my mom all the more determined as she attended every prayer meeting and evangelistic outreach in the area, asking people to pray for the salvation of her "sinner" husband. Doug happened to be in attendance at one of those meetings and she even approached him to pray.

On July 29, 1974, my dad reluctantly agreed to go with my mom to a revival meeting in the Shelbyville Chautauqua Building. I was working in Washington, D.C., but Doug was there and had a bird's eye view of watching my dad barely raise his hand, acknowledging his need for a Savior. Tears rolled down the cheeks of my family members as my dad walked forward to accept Jesus Christ as his Savior and Lord. Miraculously, in one year's time all seven members of my family were saved. My dad would often tell people that he was "an overdose of prayer!" Five months after my dad's salvation, he sensed the Lord calling him into the ministry. Much to the amazement of the business community, he resigned from his job to go into the ministry full time.

On October 23, 1975, my parents were asked to be guests on the Full Gospel Business Men's television show "The Way, The Truth and The Life." I was told the program would air at 7 o'clock on Sunday and assumed it was an evening show time. Some friends and I drove from Charleston to the House of Prayer just so we could watch the program with my parents. The House of Prayer had a 6 p.m. service so we got there just in time. Much to my dismay, the TV show featuring my parents was on at 7 a.m. that day! I could not believe the program had already been aired!

It just so happened that Doug came to the House of Prayer for the first time that evening. He lived in Clinton about 30 miles away and attended the Clinton Assembly of God Church. A friend told him about the House of Prayer so they decided to check out the Sunday night service. Ironically, I happened to be in attendance. I found out later that Doug took one look at me and knew I was the one for him. I, on the other hand, must not have been very impressed with him because I do not remember meeting him that night!

A couple of weeks later I came home from college and was

surprised to see Doug bounding up the staircase to the second floor of the mansion. It was a Saturday afternoon and he decided to stop by to see my parents. He wanted to tell them of his decision to leave the Clinton Assembly of God Church so he could start coming to the House of Prayer.

Still in my "women's lib mode," I made my infamous comments to him about not ever planning to get married. That must have deflated his ego tremendously! He wasn't stymied, though, by my remarks and started coming to the House of Prayer on a regular basis, playing his trumpet for the services.

In the meantime I was getting restless about my "no marriage policy" and realized that perhaps I actually needed a man in my life to be my husband. In December when I came home for Christmas vacation, I felt an urgency to have a talk with Jesus. I got down on my knees beside a chair in an unused room on the third floor. No one was around. I poured out my heart to the Lord and confessed that I actually needed someone to love plus I had the need for someone to love me. I rededicated my life to serving the Lord. And then, it was almost as though I heard an audible voice which said, "I will give you what you desire." I left the room, went downstairs and visited with my family. No one but Jesus knew my prayer.

Lo and behold, about a week later Doug asked me to go ice skating with him. It was our first date! I found out much later that he had tried to call me several times at college, but just did not have the nerve to finish dialing the number.

Doug drove us to a frozen pond out in the country near Clinton. We had a great time skating! Afterwards we stopped at a little restaurant to get some hot chocolate. That was the beginning of a whirlwind courtship.

On New Year's Eve we drove to Pekin and attended a New Year's Eve Watch Service that featured the same evangelist who led my dad to the Lord. Doug's heart and my heart were being knitted together spiritually.

I headed back to school to finish my last semester of college. I was already offered a job as a newspaper reporter when

I graduated in May. In order to complete my journalism major, I had to intern on a commercial newspaper for a 40-hour work week. During my Christmas break, I did my internship at the *Decatur Tribune,* a weekly newspaper. The newspaper's editor/publisher assigned me the task of writing a feature story about my family's ministry and its purchase of the England mansion. He hired a local photographer to take several photos during a Friday night service. We were amazed to see a front page picture of the mansion and a two-page inside spread with the banner headline "Landmark Converted into the House of Prayer." It was more publicity than my family ever dreamed possible! The publisher liked my work so well that he offered me a job when I graduated. I was the first reporter/feature writer he had ever hired!

My last semester at Eastern Illinois University was extremely busy with a full load of classes plus a Greek class from Lincoln Christian College. Extra-curricular activities also occupied a great deal of my time.

Then there was my developing relationship with Doug. He started writing me love letters and came to visit me as often as possible. Everything was happening so quickly! I was totally unprepared when he drove me to Charleston's Morton Park and asked me to marry him. He opened up a white ring box lined with blue velvet and put on my left ring finger a diamond engagement ring. It was beautiful! Instead of having a solid gold band, it had a unique cut-out flower design on both sides. Doug was told it was one of a kind. The wedding band had a small diamond and hooked into the engagement ring.

I was as excited as I could be and told Doug yes. The ring was actually too big for my finger so I wore it on my thumb until we could get it sized smaller. There would be another time in my life when I would wear a special ring on my thumb.

My Christian college friends were happy for me, but skeptical about me getting a ring so quickly. Did I really know Doug well enough to marry him? I didn't care—I was in love! There was no doubt in my mind that God had brought us together.

In February Decatur's Gates Bridal Shop had a once a year sale. I tried on several gowns and ultimately decided on one that was marked down to $60. I found a veil I liked for only $15. Who would ever dream I could get the whole bridal outfit for only $75?

We set August 7 as our wedding date. I told Doug I needed to concentrate on my studies and would make the rest of our wedding plans after I graduated in May. He agreed.

Everything seemed to be going well. Doug got hired by the Decatur Public Transit System as a bus driver. My parents told him he could move into one of the apartments at the House of Prayer so he did not have to commute from Clinton every day. Somehow I managed to complete my studies and graduated with honors in early May of 1976.

In addition to all of this, my engagement picture and write-up were in the newspapers. I was getting married and I was flying high! I had everything going for me. How could anything possibly go wrong?

Not long after the engagement announcement was in the paper, Doug said he needed to talk to me. It was late at night, and he informed me that he was breaking off the engagement. He just was not ready for the commitment of marriage and children. The responsibilities were too overwhelming! I was stunned! Didn't he realize I had already bought my dress and our announcement had been in the newspapers? I planned to order the wedding invitations later that week. It would be extremely humiliating! He was insistent, though, so I gave him his ring back. He walked out of the house, and I did not know if I would ever see him again. I was devastated!

I went into my bedroom, crying my eyes out and wondering where God was. Didn't He tell me He would give me what I desired? How could I face my family members and friends who were looking forward to our wedding?

I grabbed my Bible and told God that if I was supposed to marry Doug then I wanted to randomly open my Bible to the passage where Jesus was at the wedding feast of Cana. With hands trembling, I opened my Bible but instead of gazing on John chapter two, my eyes were directed to Luke 1:45, *"Blessed is she who believed that there would be a fulfillment of what had been spoken to her by the Lord" (NAMS)*.

My journey as a woman of faith had begun.

Chapter Two

Job 23:10 *"But He knows the way that I take; when He has tested me, I will come forth as gold."*

For nearly a year Doug and I did not speak to each other even though we lived in the same house. I lived in an apartment on the third floor of the House of Prayer, and he lived in one on the second floor. "Never the twain shall meet" was our motto and none of the "strategies" worked that my mom or others did to get us back together.

Since marriage did not seem to be in the plans for me, I decided to immerse myself in work as a "cub" reporter for the *Decatur Tribune*. I covered everything but especially enjoyed writing uplifting feature stories.

When Doug and I broke up, I struggled for a while in my relationship with Jesus Christ. Did He have any idea what I was going through? Why did He say, "I will give you what you desire" and then have that relationship taken away from me? Was there someone else for me? I was at that age where friends were getting married, and I was a bridesmaid in several weddings. When would it be my turn? Did Luke 1:45 really imply that I would marry Doug some day, or was it just a fluke that I opened my Bible to that verse? Did God really want me to stay in Decatur and use my talents and abilities with my family's ministry, or was I to move on and establish my career in Washington, D.C., or New York?

There was an allurement to return to Washington, D.C.

During the summer of 1974, I had the privilege and honor of working as a congressional intern in the nation's capital for Congressman Ed Madigan. It was a wonderful experience, but I struggled spiritually.

The lure and entrapment of political power and splendor in Washington, D.C., were extremely attractive. The temptation was similar to when Satan tempted Jesus, and He was shown the kingdoms of the world and all of their authority and splendor. If Jesus would just worship Satan then all of that would be given to Him. In Luke 4:8 Jesus answered Satan, *"It is written, 'You shall worship the Lord your God and serve Him only'"(NAMS)*.

God was tugging at my heart, and as crazy as it may sound, I even considered dropping out of school and becoming a missionary so He could not find me and I would not have to make a decision!

Evangelist David Wilkerson, author of *The Cross and the Switchblade*, was scheduled to speak at Mattoon's Lakeland Community College. I was curious to hear his message. I honestly do not remember a thing he said, except at the end of the evening he gave an invitation to anyone wanting to make Jesus Christ the Lord of his life. That's what I needed to hear! I made a bee line to the stage, got down on my knees, repented of my sins and asked Jesus to be the Lord of my life. I gave Him all of my talents and abilities and asked Him to use me for His glory and honor. Something was different about me after that evening! I was bubbling over with joy and had a great desire to read the Bible. I could not get enough of the Lord! He confirmed He wanted me to stay in school as I made all A's that semester.

I had actually accepted Christ as my Savior a year earlier on Thanksgiving Day in 1973. I attended a Catholic charismatic prayer meeting the night before at the urging of my mom who was always preaching to me about Jesus. I reluctantly agreed to go and for the first time in my life I listened to the words of "Amazing Grace" that was sung that night. I knew I was not saved. I studied each person's face and noticed everyone had a wonderful peace and calmness. I wanted that for my life!

It was late by the time we got home. My mom gave me the book *Ministering the Baptism in the Holy Spirit* by Don Basham. I started to read the book, but fell asleep on the living room couch. Early the next morning, Thanksgiving Day, I finished reading the book, prayed to accept Christ as my Savior and was baptized in the Holy Spirit. What a glorious day to be thankful!

Doug was also raised Roman Catholic and went to a Catholic parochial grade school. He graduated from Mattoon High School in 1967. By the time he started attending Eastern Illinois University that fall, he had dropped out of church completely. Serving God was not in his plans. Students across the country were questioning their faith in God and the United States involvement in the Vietnam War. Many were receiving their draft notices to serve in the military. Doug went before the draft board but was informed he would not be drafted because of a birth defect. He was born with two right thumbs. One had been surgically removed when he was younger, but the one that remained was permanently bent in such a way that the military personnel did not think Doug would be able to shoot a rifle very well. Ironically, he ended up playing taps on his trumpet for those who were killed in Vietnam.

When Doug graduated from college in 1971, he interviewed for music teaching jobs. School districts wanted him to teach band and orchestra at all grade levels. He decided that was too much work and hitchhiked with a friend to California. He was searching for the answers to life. He explored several religions and experimented with drugs including marijuana and LSD. He hitchhiked a second time to California.

When he got back from California, he finally secured a job selling Kirby vacuums. He barely eeked out a living. One night, in desperation because he did not have money for food or for his rent, he contemplated throwing himself into a river and ending his life.

"Christ, where are you? If you are real, then get me a job," he cried out to God.

The very next morning he had the impression that he should go to the IGA Store in Clinton, Illinois. He inquired about a job and amazingly was hired for the late night shift to help stock shelves. Every night someone in management left a radio turned on to a Christian station, but locked the office door so no one could shut the radio off. Doug had no choice but to listen to religious programming all night long! After a while, he began to examine his life and realized his need for a Savior. Drugs and other religions were not the answer. He went to a small Christian bookstore and in a back room prayed with the owner to accept Jesus Christ as his Savior and Lord. He went back to his apartment and flushed all of his marijuana and LSD down the toilet. He quit drinking and discarded all of his liquor. He literally became a new creature in Christ on July 27, 1973. *"Therefore, if anyone is in Christ, he is a new creation; old things have passed away; behold, all things have become new" (II Corinthians 5:17 NKJV ™).*

After we called the wedding off, I felt extremely lonely and had to be careful that self-pity did not consume me. I immersed myself in reading God's Word and concentrated on memorizing scripture verses. If Doug was not to be my husband, then Jesus would have to be. He would have to heal my broken heart.

Every once in a while, Doug would resurrect our relationship and acted very friendly. I tried not to get my hopes up and wondered if this was the real thing or was it going to be another let down. He said he still loved me so I kept holding onto Luke 1:45. Just as the relationship seemed to progress, it would suddenly nosedive. I did not know what to think. It was an emotional roller coaster.

I was unaware that Doug was also holding onto the promise of two scripture verses. He shared with my mom the day after our engagement was called off that God had given him two scripture verses. The first one was Proverbs 3:5-6, *"Trust in the Lord with all thine heart; and lean not unto thine own understanding. In all thy ways acknowledge Him and He shall direct thy paths" (KJV)*. The second one was Romans 9:25, *"I will call them my people, which were not my people; and her beloved, which was not beloved" (KJV)*.

Somehow God had a bigger plan and was allowing our love to be tested. It would need to be a solid, committed love for days down the road. We were like broken rocks in a rock tumbler going through the various stages to become precious jewels. The process can take many weeks and requires much patience. In really difficult cases, the rocks might need to go through each stage two or three times. Nearly every stage requires tumbling 24 hours a day for 7 days a week. From the rough grind stage to the fine grind stage to pre-polish to polish and lastly to burnishing, the rough edges become smoother and shinier. These stages cannot be rushed. It takes time to produce top quality. When complete, the rough rocks become beautiful gems.

Believers are like rocks, needing rough edges smoothed out. God can use trials and the testing of our faith to change us and mold us into new creatures of Christ. Throughout the process, God requires our trust and obedience in Him despite the difficult circumstances.

His ways are higher than our ways according to Isaiah 55:8-9, *"'For My thoughts are not your thoughts, neither are your ways My ways,' declares the Lord. 'As the heavens are higher than the earth, so are My ways higher than your ways and My thoughts than your thoughts.'"* Another passage in Isaiah 48:10 states, *"See, I have refined you, though not as silver; I have tested you in the furnace of affliction."* Even if we do not sense God's presence, He is still with us. He promises to never leave us nor forsake us. *"When he has tested me, I will come forth as gold" (Job 23:10)*.

Chapter Three

Psalm 118:24 (KJV) *"This is the day which the Lord hath made; we will rejoice and be glad in it."*

Days turned into weeks, weeks into months and months into years as Doug and I "scraped" each other inside the rock tumbler. We became more amicable as time went on and as my family's ministry expanded. I have to give Doug credit. He stayed around when anyone else in his shoes would have departed and disappeared a long time ago.

By December 1981 there was a noticeable change in Doug. He became extremely friendly with me. I did not know what to expect when he asked me to go out for dinner shortly before Christmas. We talked and it was as though we picked up where we had left off nearly six years earlier. He apologized for his treatment of me over the years. He explained there were areas in his life that needed work during those years so he set his affection on things above and not on earthly things as commanded in Colossians 3:2.

He actually wrote Colossians 3:1-2 next to what I wrote him in the Bible I gave him for Christmas 1976. That year my family started drawing names for Christmas and of all the possibilities, I drew out Doug's name and he drew out my name. Was it really just a coincidence? What do you buy the person you were going to marry and since June the two of you have not spoken? I decided the safest gift would be a new Bible and wrote in it: *"December 24, 1976, To Doug, With Jesus' love and my love. Viki"* Despite our separation, I still loved him.

In the back of my mind I wondered if Doug was like Jacob in the Old Testament who worked seven years for his wife Rachel. *"So Jacob served seven years to get Rachel, but they seemed like only a few days to him because of his love for her"* *(Genesis 29:20).* Doug was a big help to my dad and family, serving them in whatever capacity he was needed. Perhaps the longevity for the testing of our love was to ensure it would last and endure no matter what happened. Surprisingly, I never dated anyone else during the years of our separation.

Doug said he had never stopped loving me. I was still the one for him and he did not want to live without me as his wife. Something was different this time. There was a depth of maturity in both of us. We had grown up! Our faith and relationship had been tested in the fiery furnace, but we still loved each other. We were emerging from the rock tumbler as beautiful jewels.

As Christmas approached, all eyes were on us. Everyone was watching to see what would happen next with "Romeo." On Christmas Eve we had a Candlelight Communion Service at the House of Prayer followed by my family's traditional gift exchange.

Later that evening after all of the festivities, Doug asked me to go for a walk. It had snowed and was absolutely beautiful! While walking hand-in-hand, he asked me to marry him again. This time it was for real! He still had my original engagement and wedding rings. I always wondered if they were still in his possession. With great enthusiasm I replied yes. The engagement ring went back on my ring finger—home where it belonged. Wedding bells were going to chime!

We selected April 3, 1982, as our wedding date. It had to be planned when my brother Kirk and sister Chris would be home from traveling with the End Time Harvesters, a Christian drama ministry that Kirk founded when he graduated from Christ for the Nations Institute. I did all of the bookings for their tours. We did not have much time to plan a wedding, but with God's help and favor everything came together. Besides,

I already had my wedding dress!

After looking at numerous wedding invitations, we settled on one that was most appropriate for us. On the outside it had in beautiful gold lettering: *"This is the day which the Lord hath made; we will rejoice and be glad in it" (Psalm 118:24 KJV).*

The wedding was performed by my dad at the Decatur Foursquare Church because the House of Prayer could not hold all of the people. Family members and friends started clapping when Doug finally kissed me as his bride and we were introduced as Mr. and Mrs. Doug Scherer. Everyone was ecstatic that we finally tied the knot!

As we approached our first Christmas together as husband and wife, we realized our marriage was a precious gift. We learned not to take each other for granted. I respected Doug and he loved me unconditionally. It was God's plan all along for us to be together—He had given me what I desired and I was still the one for Doug, his beloved.

Chapter Four

Ecclesiastes 3:11 *"He has made everything beautiful in its time."*

By the fall of 1982 I was arranging tours for two teams of the End Time Harvesters who were ministering through drama throughout the United States and Canada. The following year one of the teams spent three months ministering in Australia and New Zealand, sometimes doing as many as three to four services a day. They ministered to over 10,000 students in public schools and were allowed to give altar calls.

Before the team headed overseas, the House of Prayer Ministries, Inc. published Kirk's book *Harvesting the Field*, a "how-to" Christian drama book which included three skits, and my mom's book *Fortress on a Hill*, which was my family's testimony. We had no idea the popularity of the skits would result in the ministry eventually publishing five skit books: *End Time Harvesters Skit Book #1, End Time Harvesters Skit Book #2, Harvest Time, Gleaning for God* and *The Last Roundup*. The ministry also published *Toyland* which contained five Christmas plays. People across the country and in Canada said we had the best Christian drama material available.

In addition to booking both drama teams and overseeing the books' publication, I also arranged evangelistic outreaches across the country for my parents. The demands for arranging all of the tours plus publishing the books became a full time job, so I resigned from the *Decatur Tribune*, having worked there eight years.

Doug and I were not getting any younger and decided it was time to start a family. On January 14, 1985, I announced to everyone that I was pregnant. On August 13, 1985, Doug proudly cut the umbilical cord for our firstborn, Michael Douglas Scherer, who weighed 4 pounds, 7 ounces and was 17 ¾ inches long.

"He's awfully small, but he's wiry. He'll make it," remarked the doctor.

I tried to nurse Michael, but he was too little. Jaundice set in, and he ended up staying in the hospital while I was released to go home. He could not drink out of a bottle and started losing weight, so a tube was placed down his nose for him to be fed. He finally started to take a bottle—the size of a doll bottle.

The nurses were astonished when our family doctor said we could take Michael home five days after his birth. Usually a baby has to weigh at least 5 pounds before he can be released, but Michael only weighed 4 pounds 6 ounces.

"This is your first baby, and your parents live in the same house as you, so they can help," my doctor remarked.

Doug's parents, Jim and Sue Scherer, came from Mattoon late that Sunday afternoon to see their new grandson. Grandpa Jim finally got to hold baby Michael. He took one look at his long skinny fingers and proclaimed, "This boy will be a piano player." For several months a blue mark shaped like a music note was visible at the bridge of Michael's nose.

Because of Michael's low birth weight, we were entered into the hospital's High Risk Infant Registry Program. I was asked dozens of questions as to why Michael might have been small and born early. Nothing applied to our situation. I was informed that Michael would not do well academically and would be slow to accomplish motor skills and tasks. He would be behind other students. I was devastated! That was not something I wanted to hear about my first child. Doug and I dedicated Michael to God and prayed for His grace and wisdom in raising this bundle of energy from heaven.

When the Harvesters came home from Australia, we decided to go down to one drama team traveling full time. It was getting harder and harder to find quality individuals who could handle the demands of touring and the stress of staying in different people's homes all the time.

Changes were also happening at the House of Prayer. We needed a bigger facility to hold church services. Pastor Don Etnier from Bethel Tabernacle approached my dad and asked him to take over his church, but he was not interested. Don went away on a fishing trip and when he came back he felt impressed to ask us again about the church. We decided to go see it and were amazed to find a 150-seat sanctuary with theater seats, 10 Sunday School classrooms, a nursery, fellowship hall with a full kitchen, youth recreation room and a two-bedroom apartment behind the sanctuary.

My dad and I decided to put out a "fleece" like Gideon in the Old Testament. If God wanted us to have Bethel Tabernacle, then three things would need to happen. First, the congregation would have to agree to change the name of the church to Harvest Christian Center. Second, the church would have to get a parking lot because church members could only park on the street. Lastly, the House of Prayer would need to be paid off because we could not afford the expenses of operating two buildings.

On Sunday, July 13, 1986, members of Bethel Tabernacle were going to vote for my dad to become the pastor and for the church to change its name to Harvest Christian Center. At 1:50 a.m., while everyone was sound asleep at the House of Prayer, there was a tremendous crash in the driveway.

We quickly went outside and were horrified to find the driveway, south porch and front yard looking like a war zone. Hand carved stone pillars, a huge cornerstone, stone railings and bricks were strewn everywhere. The driveway portico was heavily damaged. A smoldering car was upside down and facing the opposite direction. A steel beam landed on top of the car. Then we agonizingly noticed the body of a young man dead in the back seat. We were up all night dealing with this devastating situation.

It was already going to be an emotional morning with the vote on merging the two church bodies and forming Harvest Christian Center. Now we had the additional burden of knowing a teenager had been killed in our driveway. How in the world could God work good out of the accident?

My dad was unanimously elected to be the pastor and the church was renamed Harvest Christian Center. God had won a tremendous victory and was preparing the way for a future association with the Etnier family!

For several days after the accident, we had teenagers come to the house to pay their last respects to the boy who was killed. Some left flowers on the driveway rubble. We witnessed to many young people and to the boy's family members.

Back and forth we dealt with our insurance company about the damages from the accident. Finally, just before Christmas, the House of Prayer Ministries received a settlement check for the damages and we used the money to pay off the House of Prayer. What a wonderful Christmas present!

Also around this same time my dad checked with the city about the empty lot across the street from Harvest Christian Center. He was informed that we could have that land for a parking lot if we would just pay $300 in back taxes. Hallelujah! In less than six months, God faithfully answered our prayers regarding the fleece.

In His timing God gave my dad a plan on how to repair the damage done by the accident. Brick by brick and stone by stone, the work got done. My dad decided to remove the hand carved stone pedestals from the mansion's seldom used north porch and transplanted them to the south porch. This removal would catch the eye of one of God's chosen people years later. Brick columns were made, concrete railings were repaired and the portico was restored.

When asked how he ever managed to get the job done, my dad grinned widely and replied, "I had a great Carpenter who showed me how."

He truly made everything beautiful in His time!

Chapter Five

Psalm 127:3 *(NKJV™)* *"Children are
a heritage from the Lord."*

With two churches coming together to form one body, it was increasingly apparent that more time was needed to help meet the needs of the congregation. At the same time, God was closing the door on the ministry of the End Time Harvesters. The Fall 1986 tour was the last one. It was time to concentrate on growing Harvest.

Doug, Kirk and I went on a Pastors/Church Leaders' tour to Israel in February 1987. We felt a tugging in our hearts to go on the trip. We had an awesome time in God's beautiful holy land, walking where Jesus walked. Our Bibles "came alive" and we were not the same after we came back. Doug and I resolved to save our money and go back to Israel sometime in the future.

With my "biological" clock ticking away, we decided it was time to expand our family. On February 8, 1989, during a blizzard, Sarah Joy Scherer was born. She was a month early, but thankfully weighed 6 pounds and 3 ounces. She would be daddy's little girl. We believed God had a wonderful plan and purpose for her life.

Like many premature babies, Sarah had major problems with jaundice and almost had to have a complete blood transfusion because her bilirubin count was very high. She stayed in the hospital eight days. For a second time I experienced the terrible emotions of going home and leaving a baby behind.

Sarah's immunity system was not developed very well, so she constantly battled ear infections which almost led to deafness. At six months she had tubes put in her ears. She got very ill with Respiratory Syncytial Virus (RSV). The biggest concern was when our family doctor noticed a premature closing of her fontanel--a condition called craniosynostosis. A baby is born with a "soft spot" on top of his head, and it usually remains open until he is 18 to 24 months old. This allows normal brain and skull growth. If it closes too early, then severe retardation and brain damage can occur as well as disfiguration of the face. Skull x-rays were ordered for Sarah who was exactly seven months old.

When I came home from the doctor's office, I prayed for a miracle while rocking Sarah. It was as though I heard an audible voice that said, "I am the Lord that heals you."

Several days lapsed before the doctor's office finally called and said the x-rays revealed everything was normal. God had done a miracle! In Hebrew Sarah means princess and she would become our beautiful princess!

There were also health issues in Doug's family. In May his brother called to tell us that their mother was diagnosed with Amyotrophic Lateral Sclerosis (ALS), often known as Lou Gehrig's disease. Lou Gehrig was a baseball player for the New York Yankees and was the first person with notoriety who was diagnosed with the disease in 1939. We had never known anyone with that disease. It was first identified in 1874 by the French neurologist Jean Martin Charcot.

ALS is a progressive neurodegenerative disease that attacks nerve cells and pathways in the brain and spinal cord, resulting in muscle weakness and atrophy. Not only are the limbs and trunk of a person affected, so are the muscles that control vital functions such as speech, swallowing and breathing. Patients in the later stages of ALS are oftentimes totally paralyzed, yet in most cases, their minds remain unaffected.

We learned that every day an average of 15 people are

diagnosed with ALS—more than 5,600 people per year. It is considered a mid-life disease with the most common age of onset in the mid 50's; however, it can develop as young as 20 years of age and well into the 80's. The average life expectancy of a person with ALS is two to five years from the time of diagnosis. Up to 10 percent of the cases are familial whereas 90 percent do not have a genetic predisposition. Sadly, we were informed there is no cure.

Doug and I did not get to see his mother very much because Sarah was only a few months old and was sick a lot. Sue's ALS continued to progress, and on September 13 we received word that she died. All of the family members concluded ALS was a terrible disease and did not wish it upon anyone. Now our children were without either one of their Scherer grandparents. Doug's father had died of a brain aneurysm in November of 1986.

When everything was settled with Sue's estate, Doug inherited some farmland in Sullivan. As a young boy at the age of 10, he felt some day that land would be his. We thanked God for this wonderful provision and used the income for the education of our children.

I was blessed to stay home with Michael and Sarah when they were very young but the time came when I needed to go back to work to help with all of the expenses of a growing family. As parents we felt strongly about helping our children discover their talents and abilities and assist with their development. I was blessed to get hired by Northwest Christian Campus where Michael and Sarah attended grade school.

It was apparent at a very young age that Michael was gifted in music. At his first piano lesson he sat on the teacher's piano bench and told her he wanted to play the classics. I thought she was going to fall over! She never had a student quite like Michael. Whenever we bought him a new music book, he would sit down and play every song in it. If a song did not sound the way he thought it should, then he would redo it. I knew then that some day he would compose and arrange music.

We assumed Michael would play the trumpet like his dad when he started band in fifth grade. We were ready to purchase a trumpet when the band director called and asked if we would consider letting Michael play trombone. He already had several trumpet players, but really needed a trombonist—someone who was already familiar with music. We agreed with his assessment and purchased a second-hand trombone. In the long run, that music teacher did Michael a favor regarding his future musical career. There were lots of trumpeters, but few trombonists.

Instead of music, Sarah ventured into sports and school leadership. She did tumbling and was on the YMCA Gymnastics Team. She discovered she really liked soccer and eventually became a referee for the Saturday YMCA soccer games. In high school she played soccer and tennis plus got involved with Student Council and numerous other extra-curricular school activities.

Doug and I learned not to take anything for granted. Michael and Sarah were a gift from God and we dedicated them back to Him. At night we prayed for them, read the Bible to them and concluded with the blessing of Numbers 6:24-26, *"The Lord bless you and keep you; the Lord make His face shine upon you, and be gracious to you; the Lord lift up His countenance upon you, and give you peace" (NKJV ™).*

Chapter Six

Ecclesiastes 3:1 *(NKJV™)* *"To everything there is a season, a time for every purpose under heaven."*

Around the beginning of 1992, Doug's Aunt Kathleen Szachnitowski, his mom's sister, started having a persistent sore throat, her speech was becoming difficult and she sounded "croupy." Her family asked the doctor if she had ALS like her sister. He replied no because the disease is not hereditary. She continued getting worse, and then on June 11 her family's fears were confirmed when she was officially diagnosed with ALS.

Unlike Sue whose onset of ALS was with her limbs, Kathleen's was a bulbar onset with speaking and swallowing difficulties. Kathleen was given three years to live. She died exactly three years to the day—on June 11, 1995.

It was uncanny to have two family members die of ALS. According to statistics, most cases were sporadic, not familial. What was the probability that someone else from the family would get it?

My dad had his own health issues, suffering with emphysema and adult asthma for three years. He almost died in 1992 but by God's grace he lived, allowing us the opportunity to name my brother Kirk as the senior pastor of Harvest Christian Center. We were able to transition responsibilities to him for both Harvest Christian Center and the House of Prayer Ministries.

On March 19, 1993, my dad went home to the Lord. My mom was a widow at the age of 59. We continued living at the House of Prayer, but by Labor Day weekend of 1994, I knew we had to sell the mansion. We could no longer afford all of the expenses, especially the high power bills. Only five people were living there—Doug and me, our two children and my mom.

There are seasons in our lives and my family's usage of the House of Prayer mansion was diminishing. It had served its purpose, but now it was time to move on. Surprisingly my mom agreed when Kirk and I told her we needed to sell the house. Her health was declining and climbing three flights of stairs was challenging. Also, it was quite a chore cleaning the big old house. When the mansion sold, my mom would come and live with us. Little did we know the adventure and testing of our faith we would experience selling the mansion.

We scheduled an open house the Sunday afternoon of Thanksgiving weekend. Two people showed up early, but I told them to come back later because we weren't quite ready. In three hours we had 550 people go through the house. It was unbelievable! Most were curious and said they had always wanted to see the interior of the house. Even the couple who arrived at 1 p.m. came back and said they liked the house. It made a big impression on them.

Our hopes were high that God would provide a buyer and that we would be out of the mansion by winter. People from California, to the east coast, and from Florida made appointments to see this beautiful mansion and its exquisite woodwork. There was something very appealing about purchasing a mansion for only $159,000. Many remarked it would sell for $1.2 million in their part of the country.

We decided to host another open house at the end of March. It would only be for two hours and unlike the open house in November, there was hardly any publicity. To our amazement, we had 250 people go through the house!

After reviewing the House of Prayer's finances, I realized we only had a few more months of reserves. I cried out to God and opened my Bible to Romans 4:20-21, *"Yet he did not*

waver through unbelief regarding the promise of God, but was strengthened in his faith and gave glory to God, being fully persuaded that God had power to do what He had promised."
I held onto the promise that God was going to do something out of the ordinary and get the mansion sold.

A doctor and his wife came to see the house on June 30, and I learned they were the ones who arrived too early for our first open house. They loved the house then, but had just recently purchased a place on William Street. It was not economically feasible for them to buy another house at that time. However, while recently driving in our neighborhood, they noticed there was still a For Sale sign in our yard and decided to come take a second look. The doctor was a neurologist and the rent on his medical office had just been raised. The mansion would make a unique location for his medical practice.

In the course of our conversation while touring the house, the doctor revealed he was a Messianic Jew—a Jew who believes Jesus is the Messiah. I was so excited I could hardly contain myself! When we went outside and got to the north side of the mansion, the doctor commented there was something missing from the north porch. I took a deep breath and started to explain that the hand carved stone pillars were removed by my dad to the south porch because there had been an accident several years earlier.

Before I could proceed any further in telling the story about the accident, the doctor put his hand on my arm and said, "I already know all about the accident. My receptionist is married to the driver of the car. He has changed his life around since then. He's grown up and they are married and have two children."

I had chills running up and down my spine! I knew beyond a shadow of a doubt that one of God's chosen people was our choice as the buyer. However, opposition arose as another interested buyer wanted to make the mansion an icon for international awareness for a false religion. We received several counter offers by both men. By God's grace and favor, the doctor received the necessary approval for office zoning and bought the house for $145,000.

For a year we had been looking for a house that would provide accommodations for my family including my mom plus have an office for me to continue running the House of Prayer Ministries. We finally found the perfect place with over 2,600 square feet. It was located in a wonderful neighborhood and had only been on the market for three weeks.

We closed on both houses on August 22, 1995, and got ready for the big move. It was time to pack and say goodbye to the house where I had lived longer than any other place in my life—20 years. A new season was upon us. New roots were to be planted. Michael and Sarah would miss playing hide and seek in the big old mansion, but would make friends in our new neighborhood. Doug and I took great pleasure watching our children grow up and planned to "grow old together" in our new home, but God had other plans.

Chapter Seven

Jeremiah 29:11 *"'For I know the plans I have for you,'
declares the Lord, 'plans to prosper you and not
to harm you, plans to give you hope and a future.'"*

The years went swiftly by as our children grew up and became adults. For 15 years we attended every concert Michael was in. He played piano and trombone in the MacArthur High School Jazz Band which was named the top jazz band in the United States and Canada by *Downbeat Magazine.* During the summer of 2001, our family traveled with the MacArthur Jazz Band to Europe where band members played in several prestigious jazz festivals.

Michael was blessed with numerous awards and musical accomplishments while a student at Decatur's Millikin University. By God's grace he graduated in three years magna cum laude in May 2006 with a commercial music degree. We were immensely proud of him! We marveled how God answered our prayers as he rose above the expectations told us when he was a baby that he would not do well academically and would be slow to accomplish motor skills and tasks.

Like most parents, we breathed a sigh of relief when we got this first child through college and looked forward to getting Sarah through school. During her senior year at MacArthur High School, she was named an Illinois State Scholar and received numerous accolades for her leadership skills. She looked forward to attending Northern Illinois University in DeKalb in the fall of 2007 with plans of majoring in marketing and obtaining a minor in Spanish.

Although we had a few more years to go, Doug and I started thinking about retirement. We would work and get Sarah through college, save money for our "golden years" and then travel. In the year 2000 I began working as a substitute teacher in three school districts. Some classrooms were very challenging, but I recognized the need for Christians to work in the public school system. By God's grace, He opened doors for me to pray with teachers, principals and other staff members.

Substitute teaching allowed me the flexibility to take care of my mom's medical needs and not be penalized if I did not work. I greatly enjoyed the interaction with students and staff. Sometimes I had as many as 10 phone calls a day to substitute teach.

Doug and I were actively involved at Harvest Christian Center teaching Sunday school classes and Bible studies. We both served on the church board. Doug played his trumpet during the services, and I wrote and printed the church bulletin every week. We went on mission trips as a family. Doug was affectionately given the title "Uncle Dougie" by the teenagers who accompanied us on those trips. They would just laugh at his stories and antics but grew to love and respect this unique man of God.

We celebrated our 25th wedding anniversary on April 3, 2007, and had an open house. The show stopper was a plaque that Michael and Sarah designed for us. It had a picture when Sarah was about three years old, and Michael was six, with the following inscription: *"Mom and Dad, Thanks for deciding to keep us and not give us up for adoption! Happy 25th Anniversary. We Love You, Michael and Sarah.*

We continued celebrating our silver anniversary with a trip to Israel in June, traveling with Zola Levitt Ministries. We were always on our soapboxes telling someone about Israel, the apple of God's eye. A misconception that many people have is that Israel is a large country, but in actuality it is the size of New Jersey. It is an absolute miracle that it is even in existence.

Over the years Doug and I supported several Messianic

Jewish ministries and believed God blesses those who bless Israel and His people according to Genesis 12:3, *"I will bless those who bless you, and whoever curses you I will curse; and all peoples on earth will be blessed through you."*

In Psalm 105:8-11 God confirms His promise that the land of Israel belongs to the Jews for a thousand generations. *"He remembers His covenant forever, the word He commanded, for a thousand generations, the covenant He made with Abraham, the oath He swore to Isaac. He confirmed it to Jacob as a decree, to Israel as an everlasting covenant: 'To you I will give the land of Canaan as the portion you will inherit.'"*

Doug fell down in Israel a couple of times, but we did not think too much about it because the terrain can be rough. Israel was "home." The only thing Doug wanted to purchase on this trip was a big shofar. We purchased a small one during our first trip in 1987, but he wanted a big one to demonstrate his trumpet playing abilities. Everywhere we went in Israel, he attracted crowds of people when he tried different shofars. He was pleased when he found one that could produce several sounds. My special gift was when Doug purchased for my birthday a beautiful silver necklace that had a cross in the center of a Star of David. It would always remind me of Doug's love for me and God's love for Israel.

By the time we returned to the United States, we were convinced that when we retired we wanted to take people to Israel on tours. We wanted people to experience Israel like we did. Zola Levitt always said that one trip to Israel was equivalent to 10 years of Sunday school.

We were not home from Israel very long when we left on another trip. Doug, Jennifer Allen from church and I drove to Nashville, Tennessee, to participate in The Call at Titan Stadium. It was based on Joel 2:15. *"Blow the trumpet in Zion, declare a holy fast, call a sacred assembly."* Sixty thousand Christians from all over the U.S. spent the day praying and fasting for repentance, for our country, for the youth, for Israel and for abortion to become illegal.

The date was July 7, 2007, which also happened to be Doug's 58th birthday. He brought his big shofar because the only thing he wanted for his birthday was to be one of the 300 men in Gideon's Army blowing their shofars at The Call. He ended up being number 297! It was an awe-inspiring moment as the sound of shofars reverberated across the stadium in the evening. We committed our lives in service to God and to be used by Him in a great way to bring others into the Kingdom through salvation in Jesus.

In September Doug and I drove to Lancaster, Ohio, to attend the Days of Elijah Conference, organized by Messianic Jewish singer Paul Wilbur. One of the speakers was Dr. Jeffrey Seif from Zola Levitt Ministries with whom we had just been with in Israel. We left there with an even greater appreciation for Israel and God's chosen people. What plan did He have in the making and why did He allow us to make three trips that year?

At the end of July, Doug and I noticed that he was having muscle twitching and quivering in his arms and chest. We did not think too much about it. Subconsciously, we probably thought that if we ignored the fasciculations, they would go away.

On September 29 while getting dressed to go to a wedding, Doug had difficulty tying his tie. It was bizarre! He had taught several of Michael's friends when they were younger how to tie a tie. Why, all of a sudden, couldn't Doug tie his tie? He fell in Decatur's Nelson Park and I saw him fall in the house. Something was wrong.

Always good about fulfilling my "honey do list," Doug had a hard time doing some chores. It took him forever to clean the outside of our kitchen cabinets. His hands got tired and he was fatigued. He noticed the fingers on his left hand were going numb. One time at a union rally he was asked to hold a placard, but his left hand could not hold the sign and kept pulling away. After that he noticed he dropped things.

I decided to do some "investigative reporting" and got on

the internet to do some research. In my spirit I already knew what the verdict was going to be. Aware of Doug's mom and aunt's diagnosis of Amyotrophic Lateral Sclerosis, I immediately went to several web sites dealing with that disease. Every symptom that Doug was experiencing confirmed he had the disease. How could a loving God permit such a horrible disease? Why Doug? He was the good guy, always willing to help others. I was devastated!

I dreaded telling Doug my suspicions but knew it was time to face reality. I told him he needed to see our family physician. He agreed and told me he had been tripping and falling, sometimes when he got on and off his bus. I was majorly concerned he would get hurt, especially if he fell when he walked from the bus station to the transit parking lot. That jaunt had him crossing a major road in our city which was heavily traveled.

When our doctor learned that Doug's mom and aunt died of the disease, his cheery countenance changed. Big red flags were raised and he suddenly knew what we were facing. He basically confirmed the disease, but ordered blood work and a brain MRI plus referred Doug to a neurologist.

We told Michael the news. He was in disbelief! Michael lived at home with us while he got his music career going including the formation of DreamVizion Productions. With a heavy heart I called Sarah, who was 170 miles away from home in her dorm room and about to receive the worst possible news. Just as I suspected, her reaction was one of absolute shock. She started crying. It was emotionally upsetting that I was not there in person with her. I felt horrible and tried to console her as best I could.

The next day Doug had blood work done, and the following week, a brain MRI. I was an emotional wreck, crying out to God constantly. We got the test results back on October 15. Doug's brain MRI was normal and all of his blood work was normal. Sarah said over and over again, "It's a miracle." We had everyone praying. Maybe it was not ALS after all.

Doug saw the neurologist on October 30. When asked

if he remembered the first time he fell, Doug replied that it was in December 2006 after Decatur's terrible Thanksgiving weekend ice storm. He had gone to the lot across the street from Harvest Christian Center to cut some of the trees that had fallen down. The chainsaw got stuck and when he went to find something to release it, he tripped and fell. He went flat on his face and bent his glasses. Thank God he was not carrying the chainsaw when he fell. That was the first of several trips he made to get his glasses fixed after falling.

The neurologist administered an EMG (electromyography) procedure which shows a muscle's electrical activity and can show abnormal movement. It is an invasive test where needles are placed through the skin into the muscle. He also had a NCV (nerve conduction velocity) procedure which is the time it takes for electrical impulses to travel the length of a nerve. The neurologist scheduled a cervical spine MRI for November 5, and then on November 8 we would meet back in his office for the diagnosis.

I continued substitute teaching, and Doug continued driving a bus. On November 2 we contacted family members to give them a heads up about his symptoms and potential diagnosis. They were in absolute disbelief! How could this disease strike a third person in the family?

The afternoon of November 4 was beautiful so Doug and I drove out to Nelson Park and walked along Lake Decatur. We prayed for God to send rain because the lake was three feet below normal for the water level. We then walked over to the flower garden. I asked Doug if he could do it all over again, would he marry me.

"Why certainly! I love you and I have always loved you. Somehow we are going to get through all of this with God's help," he lovingly told me as he held me in his arms. That was the assurance I needed to get me through the days ahead. I was going to have to be strong and would need God's strength to see me through.

The next day he had the MRI of his cervical spine. I was

annoyed with all of the tests Doug had to undergo. It was rather obvious that he had ALS, but the doctors had to order them so as to rule out any other possible disease. On November 6 I had my annual physical and my family doctor informed me that he had received a letter from the neurologist. The test results confirmed that Doug had ALS.

When we saw the neurologist on November 8, it was just a matter of formality when he gave Doug the official diagnosis of ALS. We all knew the verdict ahead of time. In the Bible, the number eight signifies new beginnings. For us November 8, 2007, will always be the beginning of a significant change for our family. The neurologist said Doug could continue driving a bus, but he did not know for how long.

He prescribed Rilutek which is the first effective treatment for people with ALS. Laboratory studies suggest that Rilutek is "neuroprotective," which means it protects nerve cells from damage. I about fell over when I went to the pharmacy to have the prescription filled and was told it costs $989 for a 30-day supply. We did not even have that much money in our checking account! Praise God, our insurance paid all but $30. That was the first of many blessings God provided for us. It was also an indication of how expensive this disease was going to be.

It was obvious that Doug had limb onset ALS like his mother where the initial symptoms of muscle weakness were in the arms and legs. The more I read about ALS, the more I became consumed with fear. I did not like how the disease progressed.

Many cried at church when we announced the news. We would need their prayers and support more than ever. In a few cases ALS stops progressing and in a small number of cases the symptoms have reversed. That was going to be our prayer. Nothing is impossible for God. He is the divine healer. We clung to those promises.

That afternoon we had a flat tire on our van and Doug was incapable of changing it. This was the first of many instances where I called upon our good church friends Craig and Kathy

Patient to help us. Doug used to be the person to help others, but now he was the one in need.

On Monday when Doug finished driving his bus route, he was given papers by bus management to see the doctor at the Corporate Clinic. Word had gotten out that Doug was diagnosed with ALS and Transit needed to know if Doug was fit to drive. There was a huge liability issue at stake. One positive note on that day was the bus drivers approved a new contract. They had been without a contract for many months. They received a nice hourly wage increase and would receive back pay from the time when the contract expired.

On Tuesday I met with a Transit official, and we talked about our options. He assured me that Transit would do everything possible to help us. The possibility of Doug returning to work depended on the decision by the corporate doctor. Doug had worked 31 years driving for Transit and only had one sick day. He had an impeccable driving record! He was at the top with seniority and had an incredible work ethic. He was dependable, on time, nearly always accepted working overtime and had a great rapport with his passengers. Transit said he was eligible for six months short-term medical disability payments. In addition he could apply for Social Security Disability, but it would take several months before it started.

When the corporate doctor examined Doug, he asked him questions about his ALS. The doctor explained that ALS can change quickly and consequently there was a safety issue with Doug's driving. Doug admitted that his left hand was getting weaker and he did not have the strength to pull up the brake. Sometimes he had to use his right hand to pull up the air release valve. There was also the issue of him tripping and falling.

"Transit cannot take a chance and have an accident occur," the doctor emphasized.

We knew that as well and did not want anyone to be harmed. As a result, the doctor wrote on Doug's paper work that he no longer qualified for IDOT (Illinois Department of Transportation) certification. He was not fit for the duty of commercial transport. He could still drive his car, but would not be able to renew his CDL license when it expired next July. At that moment the realization hit us that Doug's driving career was instantly over. Who would have ever anticipated such a drastic change in our lives?

The next day Doug gave the paperwork to Transit management. Everyone was crying. It was a shock to the bus company and to Doug's fellow drivers. I was extremely concerned about our finances. How could we make it financially without the income of the major breadwinner? How could we pay for Sarah's college education? The last thing I wanted was for her to worry about money. She had enough on her plate with college classes and a tremendous concern for her dad.

Since the contract was settled, Transit said Doug would get back pay that would help us financially. What was so crazy was that if Doug had been able to continue working, he would have made the most money ever. In addition, he and the bus company would have contributed the most money toward his 401(k) pension plan. All of that was abruptly ended.

On the positive side, God was looking out for us when Transit said that Doug was eligible for his five weeks' paid vacation. I decided to spread out those payments in January and February. Doug had accumulated 69 incentive hours for which he would be paid. I was given paperwork to fill out for Doug to receive short-term medical disability payments. The net weekly income for those payments would be $193.93. He made more than that in a day when he worked four hours overtime. Even though it was not much, it was still better than nothing. Somehow we would survive.

One of the bus drivers asked if the drivers could do a benefit dinner for us. I said no, but later got to thinking the one thing we really needed was a snow blower. Doug would no longer be able to shovel snow. Everything now depended on me. At the annual bus employees Christmas party, we felt like honored guests as the drivers and mechanics hugged us and said they were praying for us. They presented Doug and me with a card containing several hundred dollars so we could buy a snow blower. They also gave him a "retirement party" and presented him with $100 and a plaque displaying his hole puncher.

I called a friend who worked at the Social Security Office and we discussed our situation. She urged me to apply soon for Doug to receive Social Security Disability. If approved for payments, a person cannot work for six months while waiting to receive them. That would mean Doug could not work December through May and would be eligible for his first payment in June. It was hard to think that far ahead, but I had to stay one step ahead of this disease. I learned that ALS is the only disease that when a person starts to receive Social Security Disability payments, he also is given a Medicare card to help with all of the medical expenses and equipment needs. The normal waiting time is 24 months to start Medicare. Again, that was another blessing of God's provision.

Doug and I spent several hours filling out the 12 page application for Social Security Disability online. It was very involved, but we finally finished and submitted the application. It was 5 ½ weeks before we were notified that he was approved for both Social Security Disability and Medicare. His payments would be half of what he made a month driving a bus. On December 14 he was finally approved to receive the short-term medical disability payments.

At the Decatur Trades and Labor Christmas dinner, Doug won the James H. Ragan Award for his volunteer work. It was quite unexpected and a blessing to know that Doug's "behind the scene" volunteerism was being honored. As Doug walked up to accept the award, I am sure people thought he was drunk because he staggered and was unsteady. He had not drunk any alcoholic beverages in nearly 35 years. His legs were weakening from the ALS progression, causing the walking difficulty.

I was overwhelmed with everything and felt I had to work to help pay the bills. I accepted nearly every substitute teaching job I was offered. Emotionally I was a wreck. I cried on my way to schools, at the schools and on my way home. I was a "basket case" and immensely burdened. I could not see day-light. I considered doing a job change and working somewhere full time so I could bring home more income. I prayed and read my Bible, but did not have any relief. Where was God? Didn't He care what we were going through? Why did Doug have to suffer? On top of all of this, Christmas was coming and I wondered how we could afford to buy any presents. Out of the clear blue we were blessed when someone sent us a check for $400 which I used to buy Christmas presents. Teachers and staff at Warrensburg-Latham School District also surprised me with a money gift for Christmas.

Jesus said in Matthew 11:28-30, *"Come to me, all you who are weary and burdened, and I will give you rest. Take my yoke upon you and learn from me, for I am gentle and humble in heart, and you will find rest for your souls. For my yoke is easy and my burden is light."* I was carrying everything on my shoulders, trying to do everything in my own strength. I was desperate for relief. To be honest, my trust in Jesus had waned to an all time low. How could I trust Him when our world had just turned upside down? I felt like I was looking at death face-to-face.

I was completely consumed with anguish. In desperation one afternoon I poured out my soul to Jesus. I felt like Hannah in I Samuel chapter one when she cried out to God, in great grief. I told God that I could not do this alone. I needed Jesus to help me, to give me wisdom in making right decisions and strength for each day's tasks. I surrendered my burden and asked for His will to be done in our lives.

Suddenly, a peace that surpasses all understanding encompassed me. It was as if Jesus was standing next to me and spoke these words, *"'For I know the plans I have for you,' declares the Lord, 'plans to prosper you and not to harm you, plans to give you hope and a future'"* (Jeremiah 29:11).

Just as Jesus had given me the faith to trust and wait for six years before Doug and I married, He would give us the gift of faith to trust Him. He would be with us.

Chapter Eight

Psalm 9:9-10 *"The Lord is a refuge for the oppressed, a stronghold in times of trouble. Those who know Your name will trust in You, for You, Lord have never forsaken those who seek You."*

Doug's neurologist ordered physical therapy and occupational therapy for him. He drove himself to the hospital, but after a few sessions it was obvious the therapy did not help. In fact, the exercises seemed to make Doug's muscles weaker. The therapist finally said she was going to write a letter to the doctor and tell him the therapy was not strengthening him.

Simple chores became a challenge. He could not use a can opener whether it was electric or a hand-held one. What normally should only take a few minutes to change a light bulb in the bathroom shower, took Doug over half an hour. He could not raise his arms to pour seed into our bird feeders. Everything seemed twice as heavy now. At night when he went to bed, he noticed the muscle twitching and quivering spreading to his stomach and legs. Sometimes he had painful muscle and leg cramps.

The hardest thing to give up was playing his trumpet. He had been a trumpet player for 48 years, but now he no longer had the strength to hold his instrument. He tried resting his arms on the arms of a chair to give him support while holding his trumpet, but it was to no avail. He cried, I cried and so did people at church. For the first time in 31 years he did not play his trumpet when we went Christmas caroling.

During our church's Christmas Candlelight Communion

Service, promise scripture verses are put in the offering plate and an offering is not collected. Instead, the collection plate is passed around and people draw out a scripture verse. Many times over the years the verse randomly selected by individuals was just what they needed for the coming year. Doug pulled out Jeremiah 29:11 and I drew out Psalm 9:9-10, which proved to be very appropriate for the days ahead. *"The Lord is a refuge for the oppressed, a stronghold in times of trouble. Those who know Your name will trust in You, for You, Lord, have never forsaken those who seek You."*

For Christmas, Michael and Sarah pooled their hard earned money and gave us a gift certificate for a two-day stay at a bed and breakfast inn located in St. Louis' historic Lafayette Square. We had never stayed in one so we looked forward to getting away for a nice relaxing weekend.

One of Doug's cousins encouraged me to contact the ALS Association in St. Louis. I registered with the organization and a Patient Services Coordinator was assigned to us. We always looked forward to her visits so that we could "pick her brain" about an ALS issue we were dealing with.

I was determined to keep as normal a life as possible and get out of the house as much as possible. We went to the wedding of Michael's college roommate and did something we had never done before. We danced at the reception! Doug never cared to dance but he asked me to join him on the dance floor. We were both aware that we may never have the opportunity again. Tenderly he embraced me as we slowly shuffled across the floor, his legs and feet barely able to do any dance steps. It was a memory that I will cherish forever as it took great effort on Doug's part to dance.

It is a good thing we do not always know the future. We decided to use the bed and breakfast gift certificate during the Martin Luther King Jr. holiday weekend. Doug used to do all of the long distance driving, but now I "chauffeured" him to St. Louis. In a bizarre episode of events, our 1995 Dodge Caravan was stolen from in front of the bed and breakfast. I could not believe it!

Who would want an old van? This was supposed to be our nice relaxing weekend, and now we had the stress of reporting a stolen vehicle to the police. When the officer arrived, he matter-of-factly stated that our van would probably be found within a three-mile radius of the bed and breakfast. Until then, Doug and I were without transportation. It was difficult dealing with our insurance company on a holiday weekend, but we finally got permission to rent a car—a first for me.

We were completely dumbfounded as to why God would permit the theft of our van. Even if the van was found, would it be in a drivable condition? Would we have to buy a new vehicle? Would we have to stay in St. Louis longer than originally planned? Material possessions were not a priority with us, but inside the van were some CDs that I really wanted back for sentimental reasons. For Christmas I had purchased the Bible on CD for Doug. Also in the van was a music CD we had purchased in Israel and Paul Wilbur's "Days of Elijah" music CD. In addition our winter boots were in there.

As originally planned, we spent two nights at the bed and breakfast inn and then met our wonderful friends Mark and Evvy Bowman at their church on Sunday morning. Since there was not any school the next day, we decided to spend Sunday night with the Bowmans, who lived in a St. Louis suburb. Maybe our van would be found. Sure enough, a police officer called around 6:40 p.m. and said our abandoned van was found in northern St. Louis about 10 miles away from the bed and breakfast.

Thank God, Mark knew approximately where the van was located and drove us to it. The lock on the passenger door was broken, the passenger window was down and the ignition was broken. The thief or thieves had gone through the contents of our van, but the only item they stole was my portable CD player. We came to the conclusion that maybe they were "convicted" by their actions when they saw the Bible on CDs and the Christian music CDs.

The van was not drivable so it was towed to a repair shop. The next day we got an estimate for $833, but our deductible was $500 making our "non-stressful, relaxing" journey an expensive one. What an adventure!

Despite the trials, I continued to trust Jesus. What else could I do? He provided a long-term substitute teaching position for me at MacArthur High School which provided teachers' pay. He divinely protected Sarah from a horrific crime on Northern Illinois University's campus. There was a shooting in the large lecture hall of Cole Hall the afternoon of February 14. Five students were killed and 16 injured, and the alleged shooter took his life. Sarah was supposed to be in the building taking a test, but by God's grace had gotten permission the day before from her instructor to go home to attend the visitation and funeral of a friend's father.

"It's more important for you to go home to the visitation and funeral. You don't even have to make up the test. I will just figure your grade without the test," the instructor told her.

Sarah did not see the carnage and would have never been able to leave the campus to drive to Decatur because Northern went on lock-down. NIU's President and Board of Trustees decided to cancel classes all of the following week because of the funerals for the slain students. Our hearts grieved for their families. Sarah's first year of college was being marred by tragic events. I prayed God would keep her safe physically, emotionally and spiritually.

On March 11 Doug saw his neurologist who told him to stay on Rilutek and come back in six months. He filled out paperwork for Doug to receive a handicap placard from the Illinois Secretary of State's office. It seemed crazy to resort to parking in handicap designated places. That was something for "old" people.

The next day Doug fell, bent his glasses and cut a gash above his left eye. Inwardly I moaned because I hated watching what ALS was doing to my wonderful husband. He took the tumble in stride and did not let it bother him. How far was

God going to let this disease go before He healed Doug? Everyone was praying for a miracle, especially me.

While believing God for a miracle, I knew I also had to be pro-active if the disease progressed. Making the home more handicapped accessible and having the necessary equipment were constantly in the back of my mind. Our ALS Patient Services Coordinator suggested a lift chair for Doug because of his difficulty in getting up and out of our recliner chairs. Craig Patient installed three hand rails so Doug could hold onto them while going up and down our stairs. He also put a long hand rail in the shower.

Like many faith believing Christians, I initially had the mindset that using equipment exhibited a lack of faith on my part for Doug's healing. However, I began to realize that the provision of the equipment was God's way of meeting our needs. Philippians 4:19 states, *"And my God shall supply all your need according to His riches in glory by Christ Jesus" (NKJV ™)*.

In some Christian circles, a person who is sick is judged as having sin in his life. Doug definitely was not leading a sinful life. *"Therefore, there is no condemnation for those who are in Christ Jesus, who do not live according to the sinful nature but according to the Spirit" (Romans 8:1)*.

On April 15 my mom had surgery on a very large tear on her rotator cuff. She had fallen in January while stepping outside onto our back patio steps to feed the birds and slipped on some "black ice." After the surgery, I drove her three times a week to physical therapy.

Every time I left home I was constantly concerned about Doug. I never knew when he might fall. He loved working outside and felt like he could contribute something if he did yard work. I happened to be home on April 17 when he fell in the yard. I raced outside and tried to lift him up but could not do it by myself. Thank God, Michael was home and I was able to get him to help me. I hated restricting Doug, but I told him he could no longer work outside by himself. It was too much of a risk if he fell and got hurt when no one was around. That same day a cane arrived from the ALS Association. It was like a "double whammy." His independence was being stripped as he depended more on equipment and others to get around.

Just eight days later he lost the strength to raise his arms to get dressed on his own and shave. These are the things you never expect to do for your spouse, but you do because you love him. On our wedding day we made a covenant "in sickness and in health" to take care of each other. I had never shaven a man before so it was a new experience for me. Doug flinched and I asked him if I hurt him.

"No, it tickles!" he remarked. We both laughed and tried to find some kind of humor in what could be awkward moments.

Because he needed assistance getting dressed in the mornings, I had to allow extra time for that chore before I headed out the door to go substitute teach. Doug could no longer button a shirt, put on socks or tie his shoes. He questioned whether he was becoming an invalid. One evening while helping him get undressed and get his pajamas on, he commented that I smelled like steak burgers. I had cooked on the grill earlier in the evening. I asked him how he wanted me, "rare" or "well done." The latter was his reply. We both laughed and it added some levity to our evening routine.

God was definitely our refuge and showing Himself faithful. We had to trust Him at all times.

Chapter Nine

Lamentations 3:22-23 *"Because of the Lord's great love we are not consumed, for His compassions never fail. They are new every morning; great is Your faithfulness."*

The short-term medical disability payments that Doug received were just about to end. I could hardly believe six months had already gone by. His first Social Security Disability payments would not arrive until the second week in July, although we were initially told they would come in June. During the month of May, I accepted a long-term substitute teaching position at Warrensburg-Latham Middle School but would not get paid for it until the middle of June. We would not have any income for a month. I reminded God of Jeremiah 29:11 and told Him He would have to take care of our finances because I was not going to worry about them. I had enough things to be concerned about like teaching junior high students!

I read my Bible straight through every year. On May 5th I read Lamentations 3:22-23, *"Because of the Lord's great love we are not consumed, for His compassions never fail. They are new every morning; great is Your faithfulness."* I decided this was going to be a great day and I actually had a wonderful time teaching Social Studies to the junior high students.

That evening a lady called and asked if she could come over because she had something for me. I spoke to her in March about Doug and my need for summer employment. She told me about tutoring, so I was sure she was bringing me the paperwork to apply for a job. Doug was gone attending Transit's executive board union meeting where he was the recording secretary.

I was surprised when the lady arrived at my home without any papers. She shared that her parents had died and she recently received an inheritance. She knew she was supposed to help someone and proceeded to write me a check for $1,000. I was stunned and overwhelmed with gratitude! I started to cry and explained to her my prayer from the previous day. I also mentioned Lamentations 3:22-23. It was a miracle! That money would allow me to stay home with Doug and help take care of him while waiting for the Social Security Disability payment to start.

Anyone who struggles with a disease like ALS knows there are highs and lows. The next day Doug's arms hurt. We discussed where he would like to be buried—not a conversation that I relished, but we needed to talk about it. Nothing conclusive was decided.

Doug insisted on driving to Harvest Christian Center and doing some yard work in the lot that was across from the church. He needed to use the restroom and as he walked into the church, his feet tripped and he fell in the entranceway. His glasses broke and he hit his left eye. There was no one around and he could not get up. He cried out to the Lord and later told us it was as though someone supernaturally picked him up. He then heard someone vacuuming in another part of the church, and that person took him downtown to get his glasses fixed. He ended up with a black eye and abrasions on the left side of his face.

The following Thursday he fell on his back while working in our backyard. I just happened to be home and heard a loud thud. Doug was lying on the ground. I ran outside and cried out to God to give me strength to get him up. Somehow I managed to get Doug up on his knees and then he pulled himself up onto a chair. I hated to lecture him, but I sternly told him he had to adhere to my warning of not being alone outside.

We were constantly having Craig do projects at our home

to make it more handicapped accessible. Doug tried numerous Aids to Daily Living (ADL)–some worked and some did not. Doug had difficulty grasping silverware so I purchased some pipe insulation foam and put it on the handles of a fork, knife and spoon. That proved to be awkward for Doug so he came up with a brilliant idea to buy a can of Plastic Dip® and dip the handles of our utensils until there were several layers. He could then secure a firm grip and have control when eating. Drinking straws became our friend because they eliminated the need for Doug to lift a glass to his mouth.

Not only was Doug using equipment he was unaccustomed to, I had to learn how to use various tools. A leg broke off our living room couch so I had to take the staples out and drill new holes for the screws. I did the best I could as Doug coached me. The experience made me appreciate all of the projects Doug accomplished in the past on my "honey do list."

How to pay for Sarah's college education was always in the back of my mind. Mike Shampine, a prominent union leader in Decatur had passed away, so a Memorial Scholarship was established in his name by the Decatur Trades & Labor Assembly. Sarah applied for it and was the first recipient. She won $500 toward her fall tuition at Northern Illinois University.

We were always having firsts with this disease. On June 4 for the first time I had to assist Doug getting a shower. He could not turn the faucets on and off and adjust the water temperature. Craig installed a hand-held shower head which was a huge help. On that same day while grocery shopping, I finally convinced Doug to sit in one of the battery operated grocery carts and drive it around the store. I was concerned he might fall if he tried to walk. I was thankful he could still go with me when I went grocery shopping.

Doug submitted his resignation as recording secretary for the Transit union. He could no longer write. It was a sad day for him and his fellow bus drivers. A few days later when we were running some errands, Doug saw a bus and said, "That was a good life." I asked him what was a good life and he quietly replied, "Driving a bus."

Three days later for the first time ever I helped feed Doug his cereal. Never in my life did I ever dream that I would have to help feed Doug. It was very humbling for both of us!

The Women of Faith Conference was scheduled to be in St. Louis June 13-14. My wonderful friend, Evvy Bowman, called and asked if I would like to be her guest. She explained that a Christian radio station in St. Louis sponsored a writing contest with the grand prize of attending the conference for free, having front row seats, spending two nights in the Renaissance St. Louis Grand Hotel and getting backstage passes to meet one of the recording artists. Her husband Mark had written an essay about why Evvy should win the grand prize and unbeknown to her had submitted it to the radio station. He had suffered from Lyme's Disease, and their daughter had Krohn's Disease. Evvy faithfully helped her family throughout every trial and discouraging moment. The radio station declared her the winner and she could bring a guest!

Evvy actually called several different friends to see if they would like to be her guest, but everyone turned her down. Initially she did not ask me because she was aware of the logistics in taking care of Doug. However, as she prayed about the situation, she felt impressed by the Lord to call me.

I talked it over with Doug and my family members to see if I should attend. Everyone said yes and was very supportive. They would help take care of Doug for the two days I would be gone. The conference was just what I needed! It was awesome to worship the Lord with thousands of women and listen to inspiring speakers. I do not think I ever laughed so much in all my life!

Evvy and I had a chance to have a "heart-to-heart" talk about our husbands and their health. We both knew that if they died they would go to heaven. I mentioned how I had recently prayed with a man in the Intensive Care Unit at a local hospital. He was dying and not given much hope to live. Even though he was not serving God, this man was miraculously healed. I told Evvy how ironic it was for God to touch this man and spare his life whereas God might take Doug and Mark home to heaven. We decided it was a matter of trusting God and His sovereignty.

I got home the evening of the 14th and the next day was Father's Day. In the afternoon Doug prayed a blessing just like the Old Testament patriarchs: first over Michael and then Sarah. It was a special time that I am sure they will remember the rest of their lives.

I came to the conclusion that every day is a gift from God. We were going to keep on living and doing everything we could. We had a Henneberry family reunion coming up in Chicago, and I decided it was time to borrow a wheelchair in case Doug had a hard time walking. It also meant we would eventually need a wheelchair ramp built at our home.

I checked with officials from the City of Decatur about having a ramp built, but we did not qualify for city funds because our whole household income exceeded the monetary requirements. The city building code for a ramp required a maximum of one inch slope per foot. I received estimates of $6,000 and more for the material and labor to build a ramp since our home was a tri-level and the yard's landscape included a small hill. We did not have that kind of money and would trust God to provide.

At the Henneberry family reunion, Doug was named one of the honored guests. We had a wonderful time! I was very proud of Doug who was determined to walk and not use the wheelchair. He later made the comment, though, of how weak he had gotten. Just a week later he started using the wheelchair routinely. He could not operate it so I had to push him.

On Doug's 59th birthday I could not let him renew his driver's license. The man who made a living driving a bus and was named Bus Driver of the Year numerous times could not drive any more. It was agonizing for me to call our insurance company and have Doug's name taken off our policy as a driver.

"It's terrible not being able to be independent. Not being

able to do things yourself," he remarked.

Not only was I praying about a wheelchair ramp, but I also recognized our need for a handicap van. Doug was still able to get in and out of our Dodge Caravan and his car. For now I could fold up the wheelchair and take it with us. Another decision we were contemplating was selling Doug's car. We kept praying for a miracle for Doug's healing, but at the same time I knew I had to be pro-active and plan for the future. It was possible the day might come that Doug would need to be in a power wheelchair.

Although he was able to manage steps at the present time, I wondered what I was going to do if he needed help going up or down the five steps to our bedroom. I went to a medical supply company and learned that a new stair lift costs between $3,500 and $3,900. If Doug wanted to go down the 10 steps to our home's lower living area that had a fireplace, then we would need a second stair lift. This was where we celebrated all of our family gatherings. I was beginning to understand why it can cost over $200,000 a year in expenses for an ALS patient. Making a home handicap accessible is not only time consuming when checking into equipment needs, but it is also an expensive endeavor. God knew our needs and I reminded Him of them all the time!

Chapter Ten

Philippians 4:19 (NKJV™) *"And my God shall supply all your need according to His riches in glory by Christ Jesus."*

We began to learn that God uses all kinds of people to meet our needs. He might use circumstances beyond our control and even delays to provide blessings. *"As the heavens are higher than the earth, so are My ways higher than your ways and My thoughts than your thoughts" (Isaiah 55:9).*

We received a phone call from a medical supply company about a used stair lift that we could purchase for $1,400 plus costs for any additional supplies that might be needed when it was installed. I called the store back and said we would buy it. The installation would not be for at least a week.

That same day a lady who sold nutritional products stopped by our home. She was sure the different drinks would be beneficial for Doug to combat ALS. We had well-meaning Christians across the country recommend Doug drink a certain type of water or try some other product. Inwardly, all I could think was that Doug must have been doing everything right if he only had one sick day in 31 years of work. He adhered to the adage of "eating an apple a day" during all those years of work and kept physically fit. Other Christians recommended we travel to certain destinations and have believers anoint and pray for Doug's healing. I firmly believed my family had "enough faith" to pray for a miracle. Besides, our house was still the House of Prayer.

The woman, who stopped by our home, mentioned that her church was installing an elevator and had a stair lift. My ears perked up! I called the pastor of the church and left a message concerning my interest in the lift. We got permission to see the stair lift. There were actually two stair lifts and their rails would accommodate the stairways in our home. Could it possibly be our Lord was making a way for us to acquire both of them?

About a week and a half later the pastor called and said we were at the top of the list for the stair lifts, but the church would not make a decision about them until the new elevator was completely installed and inspected. He estimated it would probably be September before that would happen. In the meantime, I canceled the order with the medical supply company about the used stair lift.

Doug's neurologist highly recommended he get registered with the ALS Clinic in Springfield because the staff there could provide much more specialized medical help. I called the clinic and learned it was actually under the auspice of the Muscular Dystrophy Association. An appointment was made for August 6 for Doug to see the ALS doctor. Over the years I had made contributions to the Jerry Lewis MDA Telethon on Labor Day weekend, not having any idea that one day my husband would benefit from their services. Money raised in Central Illinois from the telethon helped fund the ALS Clinic.

I scoured the automobile ads for handicap vans. We went to a dealer who sold handicap vans, but we could not afford any of them, not even a used one. I noticed a blurb in the ALS Association's newsletter about a 1994 Dodge Ram Van that was handicap accessible with an electric lift. It had about 107,000 miles and the price was only $1,500. I knew the lift alone was worth several thousand dollars. The van did not get very good gas mileage and had been sitting idle for about a year. The co-owner had died, and the family wanted to sell it. We decided to act quickly because we knew it would get snatched up soon.

For the first time in our marriage, we decided to buy a vehicle sight unseen. The surviving owner and her sister drove from St. Louis and met us in Springfield. They explained the van's features and proceeded to show us the electric lift's operation. Much to their chagrin, it would not work. I told them not to worry, but to follow me to the dealer who sold handicap vans. An employee looked at the electrical box that controlled the hydraulic lift and found two wires touching each other. He quickly fixed the problem and then asked if I would like for him to check the van over to see if everything was okay. What a blessing! He gave the van high marks and we purchased it!

The next day I went to the driver's license facility to take care of the title work and see about getting handicap license plates. To get them, Doug needed to sign his name on the van's title. I told the employee that he could not write his name very well. She said I would have to become Doug's Power of Attorney so that I could sign his name on it. Talk about God's timing! Just the day before I had called our lawyer and inquired about the procedure to get Power of Attorney. God was already preparing me to assume that responsibility.

I went to the lawyer's office and papers were drawn up for me to become Doug's Power of Attorney. It was one more closure to Doug's independence. From now on any papers that needed Doug's signature I would sign his name and then "Viki Mari Scherer POA."

Our niece, Chantelle Henneberry, in Miles City, Montana, invited us to her wedding. Doug really felt like we should attend. It would be very difficult for him to travel the 1,200 mile distance in the handicap van so we decided to fly. The only way financially we could afford airplane tickets was if we sold Doug's 1999 Daewoo Nubira Wagon. Honestly, we could not keep paying the insurance premiums anyway since we still owned the Dodge Caravan and now the handicap van.

We advertised the Daewoo in the local *Wheels and Deals* magazine which came out on Friday. Early that afternoon a man from Bloomington called and said he wanted a 4-cylinder car for his wife who was to start a job on Monday. He saw our ad and told us to meet him at Hickory Point Mall's parking lot. He test drove the car, liked it and gave me cash of $1,800--all of it in 100 dollars bills. Unbelievable! At first I wondered if he was an angel and then later my faith wavered as I prayed that none of the bills were counterfeit! I told Doug, "I guess we're heading to Montana!"

Doug's first visit to the MDA's ALS Clinic in Springfield was quite a learning experience. Doug's weight, height and blood pressure were taken. Doug was given a pulmonary function test to measure the strength of his diaphragm and his breathing capacity. Doug's test scores revealed a 72 percent lung capacity which was very good. The test provided a baseline for the progression of respiratory involvement, and he would have many of these tests as time went on. We discovered Doug's 48 years of trumpet playing was a big plus in keeping his diaphragm and lung muscles working well.

We gave Doug's medical history to the ALS doctor. He said it is very rare to have a mother and her sister die of ALS and emphasized that only 10 percent of ALS cases are familial. We discussed the medicine Rilutek and if it was effective. The doctor said it might prolong the life of a few patients, but for the most part the quality of life is the same for the ones who do not take it. He told Doug to continue taking it for an additional two weeks and then stop the medication. He emphasized that currently there are no medications that work for ALS, but there are lots of experimental/clinical trials. I wondered if Doug would qualify to participate in a clinical trial.

We learned that Medicare would pay 80 percent of Doug's medical costs associated with ALS. Everything with Medicare is diagnosis driven so Doug was given a script for a power wheelchair evaluation. If he qualified for one, then a wheelchair ramp at our home needed to be built to code. Medicare required a house inspection upon the chair's delivery to make sure our home could accommodate one. In addition to having the power wheelchair evaluation, Doug also needed a speech therapy evaluation. An appointment for both evaluations was made for August 27. Doug was told to come back to the clinic every six months if his ALS was stable, but if any issues arose, then he should come sooner.

That evening while sleeping, Doug had an oxygen test. A Finger Pulse Oximeter measured Doug's blood oxygen saturation and pulse rate throughout the night while he slept. Test results revealed everything was normal.

A bizarre thing happened on August 6 while I drove our handicap van to our church's evening service. Someone "randomly" threw a rock at our van and hit the back left window, shattering it to pieces. I could not believe it! Who would throw a rock at a handicap van? By God's grace Doug did not get hit by the rock or cut by the glass. He was in his wheelchair which was strapped and buckled to the van's floor.

I reported the incident to the police and talked to our insurance company the next day. I had to get the window fixed and was concerned about paying the deductible. Where would the money come for that? How could we get all of the broken glass cleaned up? When the insurance adjuster heard that we were on our way to church, she said we had Faith Guard on our policy. This meant that we did not have to pay any deductible because the incident occurred while we were on our way to church. I did not even know we had Faith Guard! What a huge blessing! The glass company replacing the window cleaned up the broken glass. Also, because the breakage was considered vandalism, our future insurance premiums would not be raised. God divinely protected Doug and was definitely looking out for us!

Our ALS Patient Services Coordinator stopped by about a week later and said we qualified for a respite care grant. The ALS Association would pay up to $1800 for six months for someone to come to our home twice a week for two hours to help take care of Doug's needs including fixing his lunch. This allowed me the opportunity to continue substitute teaching or run errands if I happened to be home. The annual Walk to Defeat ALS helped raise funds for the respite grant.

My life got even busier when Decatur's Life Central Bible Institute started its fall semester. I was a faculty member teaching the Principles of Writing II class one night a week. In addition, I got phone calls every day to substitute teach.

Outside of the house, Doug had to be in his manual wheelchair which he could not operate by himself. Getting him out the front door and into the handicap van was quite an ordeal. It was unsafe to push the wheelchair down our yard's hill to the driveway so I drove the van to our neighbor's driveway. I backed it in, opened the side doors and then let the electric lift down. In the meantime, Doug waited for me at our front door. Quickly I walked back to our house, put the wheelchair at the bottom of our front step and helped Doug down the steps to get him into the waiting wheelchair. Then I wheeled him across our yard and our neighbor's yard and got him onto the handicap lift. Once inside the van, the wheelchair had to be secured with straps and hooks so that it would not move when the van was in motion. It was a lot of work, but I was grateful I could still get Doug out. In the back of my mind I kept thinking about the approaching winter season and our need for a wheelchair ramp. The time would come when I could no longer push the wheelchair across the two yards because of snow and ice.

Doug had a swallow test as part of his speech therapy evaluation on August 27. Thankfully his swallowing muscles were still good and he was told he could eat anything he wanted. We were told about various speech devices and warned it could take a couple of months to get one approved by Medicare after a doctor's script is submitted. In the back of my mind I thought, "Doug won't need a speech device. God is going to heal him."

Doug also had his power wheelchair evaluation. The doctor needed to sign the paperwork and then there would be an insurance review. Medicare would make the final determination about the need for a chair. If approved, then the chair would be ordered and made according to the specifications needed for Doug and his ALS. It could be several months before Doug actually received the wheelchair.

We flew to Montana on August 28 for our niece's wedding. I was grateful that employees at each airport assisted me with luggage or pushed Doug in his wheelchair. My sister Chris also flew to the wedding and was a big help. Doug was a real "trouper" and greatly enjoyed the trip. I wondered if this might be our last big trip, but God had plans for one more that would give us national exposure with the disease.

About a week later while substitute teaching at MacArthur High School, I was asked by one of the teachers how things were going. I mentioned how we fell through the cracks in trying to get a wheelchair ramp built. She recommended I call the Decatur Trades and Labor Assembly or call the United Way of Decatur and Macon County and tell them about our need. She said I had subbed a lot over the years at MacArthur and since both of our children had attended there, then teachers ought to contribute money in a bucket toward the ramp. I was blessed by her suggestion, but felt awkward about receiving contributions. It was such a humbling experience dealing with ALS. Doug and I were accustomed to being on the giving end, not the receiving end.

Doug wanted to do his part in trying to help find a cure for ALS so he agreed to be in an experimental drug research at Washington University School of Medicine in St. Louis. I spoke with the Research Nurse Coordinator in the Neuromuscular Division and she said the enrollment cutoff date for the Knopp CL201 study was the first part of October. We would have to act quickly and get Doug's medical charts sent to her. If Doug was accepted into the study, then initially he would be required to make two or three trips a month to St. Louis. Eventually our travel would level off to one trip a month. Because we lived 130 miles from St. Louis, the study would pay for our mileage and for one night's lodging at The Parkway Hotel which was adjacent to Washington University Medical Research Center and Barnes Jewish Hospital. A third floor walkway linked the hotel to the research center.

One of Doug's cousins called and said she needed a photo of Doug for a brochure her family was making to raise funds for the upcoming Walk to Defeat ALS on October 18 in Springfield. The Szach Pack Team (short for Szachnitowski which was his aunt's last name who died of ALS) had green T-shirts with white lettering on the back which read "We walk for our family" and listed the names Kathleen Szachnitowski, Suzanne Scherer and Doug Scherer.

On September 21 Doug and I went to the Decatur Trades and Labor Unions cookout at the IBEW Hall. Matthew Dial was told about our need for a wheelchair ramp. His father, grandfather, great aunt and great uncle all died of ALS. Needless to say, he was touched by our situation and agreed to help us out. One of the Transit drivers was there and asked if I wanted the bus drivers to contribute financially toward a wheelchair ramp or to the ALS Walk.

"Ramp contributions would be great," I responded.

Doug's medical charts arrived at the Washington University School of Medicine. If he wanted to participate in the experimental drug research for the Knopp Study, then he needed to be in St. Louis on Thursday at 8:30 a.m. for a clinical evaluation. I was already booked to substitute teach that day so I canceled the job.

The handicap van was having problems starting, and I found out it needed a new fuel pump at a cost of $580. A month earlier we had spent $336 on a tune-up for the van and replaced several parts. That was nearly $1,000 not in our budget. It was critical to keep the van in good operating condition, especially if we were going to be making numerous trips to St. Louis.

During Doug's clinical evaluation, he was actually asked to be in three studies: 1) the Knopp Study, provided he qualified for it after his blood test results were in, 2) a genetic research study that would include our children and members of Doug's family and thereby develop a genetic marker for muscular disorders in the family, and 3) collect a skin biopsy from Doug that would be used in the laboratory to grow stem cells and eventually motor neurons. Researchers' future goal is to replace degenerative motor neurons with new ones.

Doug had a thorough physical examination, blood work and a breathing test. I signed consent forms for the biopsy and genetic study, but we had to wait until the blood results were back before the Knopp Study forms could be signed. The Program Coordinator for Neuromuscular Genetics in the Department of Neurology at Washington University School of Medicine said the research center was particularly interested in seeing if Doug carried the SOD1 gene. In 1993 this was the first ALS gene identified and is present in about 30 percent of familial ALS patients.

If approved for the Knopp Study, Doug would be asked quality of life questions on subsequent visits. These questions covered physical, emotional, spiritual, social and financial matters. He was asked how he was doing with various skills such as speech—was it normal or had it changed; did he notice any additional saliva; did he have problems with swallowing or choking; how was his breathing—did he have shortness of breath; how was his handwriting—was it decipherable; was he able to cut his own food and feed himself; was he able to shower, shave, take care of personal hygiene and get dressed; could he turn over in bed by himself; and did he need assistance with walking.

To make it easier on family members who would be in the genetic testing, they would not have to have blood drawn, only saliva collected. All they basically had to do was spit in a cup and then mail their packets back to her. None of the family members would be told if they had the SOD1 mutation because if they knew they carried the gene, it would raise their stress level. All of the information from the research would be kept under strict confidentiality. Only Doug would be told the results of his genetic testing. Researchers wanted to look for any specific linkage in the family members.

Doug and I discussed several times that we would not have wanted to know 20 years previously if he was going to have

ALS. In fact, we would not have wanted to know in 2006. If we knew Doug was going to be diagnosed with ALS in 2007, we would have never spent the money to go to Israel. We prayed that our children and other family members would not let fear of the ALS disease captivate them and hold them hostage. *"For God has not given us a spirit of fear, but of power and of love and of a sound mind" (II Timothy 1:7 NKJV™).*

The research nurse called and said Doug's blood work was okay so he could proceed with the next step in the Knopp Study which was a lumbar puncture where fluid is taken out of the spine. He did very well with the procedure and took his first dose of Knopp pills on October 7. We did not know if they were a placebo or the real thing, a high dosage or low dosage. I had to keep accurate records each time he took the pills or any other kind of medicine. Any changes in Doug also had to be recorded. His next visit was October 16 and it involved a pharmacokinetic (PK) analysis. He had 12 blood draws over the span of 8 hours.

"You brought me some wonderful veins and I appreciate that! You can just stick around all day all eight hours," remarked the nurse.

On our way home from St Louis, we stopped at a fast food restaurant. Doug went into the restroom and I followed him in. He needed help with his zipper. That was my first time in a men's restroom and it certainly would not be my last. He already had some bathroom accidents, but never complained.

In addition to Doug's health needs, my mom, who lived with me, was having her own physical battles. Doctors suspected her breast cancer was back so as a precautionary measure she had a lumpectomy on October 9. In June 1999 her left breast was removed in a mastectomy. She was blessed at that time because she did not have to have radiation or chemotherapy, but this time she did not fare as well and had to have radiation. As if my life wasn't already busy enough, now I chauffeured my mom to her radiation treatments. Many times throughout the day I quoted Philippians 4:13, *"I can do all things through Christ who strengthens me" (NKJV™).*

Miraculously, monetary donations to buy the materials for the wheelchair ramp started coming in from teachers, bus drivers, friends and churches. I was overwhelmed by their generosity! Our needs were being supplied, fulfilling Philippians 4:19, *"And my God shall supply all your need according to His riches in glory by Christ Jesus" (NKJV™).* Approximately $3,000 was raised for the ramp. In addition, I raised about $1,400 from friends and family members for the October 18 Walk To Defeat ALS that was held in Springfield.

Although we did not see any evidence of Doug being healed, we saw God's glorious provisions over and over again. Some people gave us gift cards or money to buy groceries or whatever we needed. Others brought over cooked meals. Oftentimes people sent us cards of encouragement to let us know they were praying for us. One friend worked at a thrift store and looked for clothes that would make it easier for me to dress Doug. A couple of times people mowed our yard.

It was a huge blessing to receive the funds for the ramp because our personal finances continued to take a big hit. The transmission went out in Sarah's car, and we decided to replace it rather than buy a new vehicle. Also, our handicap van had been back in the fix-it shop. We did not have a surplus of funds, but we were not going hungry and we had a roof over our heads. God was faithful!

Doug's genetic test results revealed he did not have the SOD1 gene mutation. Consequently there was some other gene in the family responsible for the ALS disease. If a linkage gene was found, no one in the genetic study would be told if he had it.

For the first time in a long time the price of gasoline was below $2 a gallon. I filled my mom's car with gas and decided at that bargain price to get the Dodge Caravan filled. I wanted a pump that did not require pre-payment. Impatiently I waited for the lady in front of me to get done. She was actually standing near the service station's building, talking on her cell phone. I was under a time constraint because I needed to get home to fix supper, feed Doug, clean up the kitchen and be at church for the 7 p.m. service. I was running late because I had taken my mom to Springfield for a doctor's appointment earlier that afternoon.

When the lady finally came to her car, I assumed she would drive off but instead she started to fill up her car. I was "fuming" and decided to drive around to the adjacent pump only to find an older gentleman filling up his SUV. When he finished that task he then proceeded to wash every window on his vehicle. I went back around and finally the lady drove off.

While I was pumping gas, a lady I knew pulled up in front of the SUV. She asked how Doug was and I said the ALS disease was progressing. When I went to pay for my gas, she was waiting for me by the station's door and said "I've got it." She paid for my fill up! I was stunned! She then asked if I could use a Thanksgiving basket. I did not know what to say! She insisted on bringing one to my home. She then said that she planned to meet me at the gas station each month so she could fill up the handicap van. I cried! I could just see every angel in heaven delaying me and preventing me from getting gas just so the timing would be perfect for this lady to show up. What a beautiful random act of kindness!

Because Doug could no longer climb the stairs in our home by himself, I prayed even more urgently for the stair lifts. I called the church that owned them and was told the elevator was used for the first time on Sunday, but it had not been inspected and was not licensed. It had taken almost three months longer than expected. The pastor planned to talk to his trustees at their Thursday night meeting where a decision would be made one way or the other. He personally wanted to give us the stair lifts, but it was not his decision. He commented that an unexpected large financial gift had recently been donated to the church for the elevator so that might help in the trustees deciding to give us the stair lifts. However, there was one trustee who wanted us to buy them. We asked everyone to pray for us to have favor.

Finally, the pastor called on November 13 and said the trustees voted to give us the stair lifts. Glory hallelujah! What a wonderful Thanksgiving present! The lone trustee who wanted us to pay for them was absent from the meeting.

Work got started on our wheelchair ramp. Fifteen holes that were 36 inches deep were dug for the posts. A big work day was scheduled for November 15. Craig Patient, Matthew Dial, his brother, a cousin and several other men from local unions showed up. Several of the post holes were filled with concrete when the guys realized their design plans for the ramp would not work. Somehow we needed an exemption from the one foot/one inch slope rule.

My uncle in Kansas e-mailed me the International Residential Code which stated an exception to the maximum slope rule. "Where it is technically infeasible to comply because of site constraints, ramps may have a maximum slope of one unit vertical to eight horizontal." One of the men helping build the ramp spoke with our city inspector who approved the exemption for us. The post holes that were already filled with concrete had to be busted out and a new plan was designed which was better suited to Doug's liking. Weather was becoming a huge factor in getting the ramp completed.

I started praying about staying home from teaching so I could take care of Doug during the coming year. More and more he required full time care. Somehow God would meet our financial needs without any of my teaching income.

The bus drivers were wonderful and brought food to help me feed the guys who were building the ramp. They also donated more money toward the ramp. In a card the drivers gave us, one of them wrote, "Doug, I'm praying your journey home will be as smooth as the ride you gave all your passengers."

Just before Thanksgiving while in a grocery store, I talked to a lady who asked me the question, "Where is God in all of this?" I shared how God was meeting our needs in wonderful ways. Despite our low income, Doug and I continued to tithe and give to missions. I mentioned my "gas angel" who planned to meet me on a monthly basis at the gas station and pay for my handicap van to be filled up with gas. I spoke about the woman who came to my home in May and wrote us a check for $1,000 not knowing I prayed the day before about our needs. I talked about the miracle of the stair lifts, the money donated for the wheelchair ramp and the wonderful volunteer laborers. She was so touched and amazed at God's provision. She commented she could not wait to tell her church our story. In the next breath she asked, "Can I buy your groceries?" What a blessing!

The next morning the work crew arrived to build the wheelchair ramp. It was cold and windy, not very conducive for outdoor work, but the guys did not seem to mind. An electric auger was rented to dig new holes for the posts. The front concrete steps and the old concrete footings were busted out. Concrete was mixed and the new holes were filled. Throughout Thanksgiving weekend the volunteers diligently worked and constructed the "mother of all wheelchair ramps." Many in the medical supply field said they had never seen a wheelchair ramp built as well as ours. Doug and I praised God over and over again for those who sacrificed their time to build it and those who gave financially to buy the materials.

We made another trip to St. Louis on December 2. Doug's weight was down to 137 pounds, but everything else looked good. He rated his quality of life as 6 out of a possible 10. He had "good veins" for the blood draw.

On December 10 the two stair lifts were installed in our home. What a wonderful provision from God! Now Doug could ride the stair lift up or down the steps and then get into his wheelchair.

The next day the power wheelchair arrived and we passed the house inspection. Lots of "bells and whistles" were on the chair to accommodate Doug's ALS needs. It was so nice not having to push Doug in a manual wheelchair and instead have a wheelchair that he could operate. It cost over $23,000 which was more than any car we had ever purchased! Our trips to St.

Louis would be much more comfortable for Doug instead of him sitting in a manual wheelchair.

Not until the last day of the year did the City Inspector come to inspect the ramp. He commented that he knew it was well built when he turned the corner onto our street and could see it in the distance. He instantly approved it!

The year 2008 came to a close and we were better equipped to combat the ALS disease. God had supplied our needs and we shared with everyone our wonderful testimonies. What would we be doing a year from now on New Year's Eve?

Viki and Doug Scherer on their wedding day April 3, 1982

Jennifer Allen, Doug (holding his shofar) and Viki at The Call in Nashville, Tennessee, on July 7, 2007

Doug (on the left) named Bus Driver of the Year in 1991

Doug and Viki in Israel June 2007

Doug, Viki, Sarah and Michael November 18, 2006

Viki, Doug, Sarah (holding Friskie) and Michael wearing Szach Pack Team t-shirts for the ALS Walk on October 18, 2008

Michael, Doug, Viki and Sarah at the October 17, 2009, ALS Walk in Springfield, Illinois

Doug and Viki on the "mother of all wheelchair ramps" at their home

Viki and Doug attending the 2009 Roadmap to a Cure National ALS Advocacy Day and Public Policy Conference in Washington, D.C.

Chapter Eleven

Proverbs 3:4 *"You will win favor and a good name in the sight of God and man."*

We were barely into the New Year when Doug developed a persistent cough and had pain on his lower left side. My neighbor, who is a registered nurse, recommended we call our family doctor even though it was late at night. He told me to take Doug to the hospital emergency room. There was concern that a blood clot may have formed, but a chest x-ray and CT scan revealed pneumonia in the lower left lobe of his lungs and also pleurisy. Levaquin was prescribed for the infection and Darvocet for the pain.

I was hesitant to take Doug the next day, January 7, for his appointment at the ALS Clinic in Springfield, but was told that if he did not come in at that time he would not be able to come until March. Doug was feeling lousy, but I got him ready for the ride to the Koke Medical Center. By the time we got there, he was sick to his stomach and vomited. One of the doctors explained that Darvocet can make a person nauseous. She said Doug needed to stop taking that medication and instead prescribed Zofran. He threw up again as we were leaving the clinic and ended up sleeping all the way home.

I was majorly concerned about Doug and prayed about what to do regarding our trip to Chicago O'Hare Airport later that evening. Sarah was scheduled to fly to Costa Rica at 6 a.m. the next morning and had to be at the airport at 3 a.m.

She was studying abroad for a semester with University Studies Abroad Consortium (USAC) to become better proficient at Spanish. Our doctor gave his approval for Doug to travel so we left Decatur at midnight.

Sarah kept in touch with us throughout her flights, so it was rather odd that she did not notify us when she landed in Costa Rica. Later that evening I received a phone call from USAC informing me that all 100 students were accounted for. An earthquake that registered 6.2 on the Richter scale had struck Costa Rica just as Sarah was checking in at the airport. Incredible! Sarah's host parents were wonderful to her and provided great accommodations! Over and over again I praised God for their kind hospitality and that their home was not damaged from the earthquake.

A few weeks before Sarah left for Costa Rica, we were notified by Northern Illinois University's Student Financial Aid Office that she was awarded a $2,500 scholarship. That money plus her MAP Grant and Pell Grant would pay for all of her tuition that semester. I was shouting "hallelujah" because I had prayed for a long time that if God wanted Sarah to go to Costa Rica to study abroad, then He would have to provide the finances.

Doug was fitted for an AFO ankle brace which would help give his right leg more support. There was always something new to learn when dealing with ALS. The same day the brace arrived was the first time Doug did not want me to put his watch on his wrist. He could not lift his arms to see the time.

While scooping snow on the driveway, I noticed we had "green" snow. The handicap van was leaking antifreeze. We ended up having to get a new radiator at the cost of $343. Thankfully it was repaired in time for our January 30th trip to St. Louis. I was grateful for Doug's participation in the Knopp Study because every time we went to St. Louis he was given a breathing test, his vital signs were checked and he was weighed. He could no longer stand on a scale, but there was a huge scale that could weigh him in his power wheelchair. The nurses subtracted the weight of the chair, and then we knew exactly how much he weighed. On this visit his weight was down to 137.2 pounds.

Doug was encouraged to get a G-tube while his breathing was still good, the sooner the better. With a feeding tube he could be assured of getting 1,500 calories a day. ALS patients burn up more calories and lose weight quicker than other people so each pound lost is very critical.

Doug ranked his quality of life that day 9 out of 10. He was told by a neurologist that he had beaten the odds for living with ALS. He pointed out the average life span is only two years and the first time Doug fell was over two years ago.

Before we left the Research Center, the Research Study Nurse Coordinator made the comment that I was a "tremendous wife."

"You are so patient. All of us have been watching. Your faith is what contributes to that. God has a plan for everybody's life and for what is happening. That's what helps me with my job. Prayer changes things," she remarked.

I was greatly encouraged and reminded Doug every once in a while that he had a tremendous wife!

Doug got a prescription from the pulmonary doctor in Springfield's ALS clinic for a cough assist machine. It was another piece of equipment to learn, but helped Doug cough so that fluids would not settle in his lungs.

We were abundantly blessed to receive a check for $1,700 from the St. Louis United Way's 100 Neediest Cases Program. I had no idea we would get that much! It was a confirmation to me that I had made the right decision to stay home and take care of Doug. God would meet our financial needs without me working. The ALS Association St. Louis Regional Chapter referred us to the program.

Applications were being accepted by Illinois State Senator Frank Watson for an Illinois General Assembly Scholarship. It would pay all of the tuition for a year at a state university. Watson required applicants to be a college junior, and Sarah had just become a junior that semester. We prayed for favor with Sarah's application. A decision on scholarship winners would not be made for a while.

Doug's right ankle was swollen from wearing the AFO so we went back to the specialist to have it adjusted. He also started having the same pain as when he had pleurisy. His legs were "jumping" all the time, he was coughing and his nose started running like a faucet. When I went outside to start the handicap van to take Doug to the doctor, the battery was dead. I had left the lights on. Thankfully Michael was home and helped me jump the van. We were only a few minutes late to the doctor appointment. Doug did not have pneumonia this time, but he did have a touch of pleurisy and an upper respiratory infection.

While waiting to get our taxes done, Doug made a comment to me in the conference room.

"I just wish I could go to sleep and not wake up."

"So you would be in heaven?" I responded.

"Yes," he softly replied.

We received word from the ALS Association St. Louis Regional Chapter that our family was selected as the family that best exemplifies "the spirit of ALS across America for the state of Illinois." We were told the "ALS Across America" National Campaign recognizes courageous individuals with ALS and their caregivers who are role models to people with Lou Gehrig's Disease. Media outlets across the state were sent a news release about us.

"These special individuals reflect the spirit of the organization as they make a positive difference in their community by expanding awareness of ALS and embodying the spirit of living life to the fullest.

"Doug and Viki are important to the chapter because Doug is a patient. Also, they give us the energy, determination, and motivation to face the challenges of managing ALS and finding a treatment or cure.

"Doug reminds us that it is not just Lou's disease, it is

everyone's disease."

It mentioned the scripture verse Jeremiah 29:11 and Doug's calm determination and faith.

"Doug has always been the person behind the scenes to quietly help others—he has a true servant's heart. It has sometimes been overwhelming for our chapter to be on the receiving end."

Doug had another appointment in St. Louis on February 13. We returned some unused medical equipment that we had borrowed from The ALS Association St. Louis Regional Chapter. I told the chapter's President/CEO that we were going to Springfield, Illinois, on March 5 to participate in the State Advocacy Day for ALS. He asked if we would be interested in going to Washington, D.C., May 10-12 to attend "Roadmap to a Cure National ALS Advocacy Day and Public Policy Conference." The ALS Association would pay our way including transportation, hotel, conference costs and some meals. We would have to be willing to talk to congressmen about our story with ALS and advocate for funding. I told him we would be thrilled to go and shared that I had been a congressional intern the summer of 1974. It would not bother me to talk to senators or congressmen on Capitol Hill!

Who would ever dream my experiences in Washington, D.C., would be beneficial for a conference dealing with ALS? In addition, my journalism background came in handy when Doug and I did TV and newspaper interviews throughout Central Illinois and in Chicago as a result of our family being selected as a family that best exemplifies the spirit of "ALS Across America."

A huge responsibility for me was keeping an accurate log of the Knopp experimental medicine that Doug was taking and recording all of his other medications. I had to keep track of each dosage, when it was given and if there was any reaction. He had a terrible problem with itching and I had to document each anti-itching cream that he tried.

"Where There Is Faith" was the title of my "sermon" that

I shared at my church during the morning worship service on March 1. I shared many of our testimonies of God's provision during Doug's illness. This opportunity made me wonder if God would open the doors for me to share with others in the future.

The next day my "gas angel" called and told me to bring to the gas station the vehicle that needed the most gas. Both our handicap van and the Dodge Caravan needed gas but I did not tell her. In the next breath she said, "I tell you what. You bring one vehicle, fill it up and I'll pay for it. Then you go home to get another vehicle and I'll pay for it also." So I did! When we got done filling the second vehicle, she made the comment, "We'll have to do this again." Wow, what a blessing!

On March 5 Doug and I went to Springfield for the Illinois ALS Advocacy Day. We met with Illinois State Senator Kyle McCarter who had just replaced Frank Watson because he was recuperating from a stroke. McCarter's scholarship committee would now be the ones to determine who would receive the Illinois General Assembly Scholarships from his office. We talked to Illinois State Representative Bob Flider, who said he wanted to co-sponsor legislation for ALS spousal caregivers to receive financial benefits. We also visited Illinois State Representative Bill Mitchell and shared our story about ALS. I was grateful Doug was in his power wheelchair as we traveled from one legislative office to the other.

I checked into flying to the nation's capitol for the National ALS Policy Conference, but I knew Doug could not walk down the aisle of an airplane. I was informed by several individuals that if he did fly, there was a good chance his power wheelchair would get damaged while it was in the plane's cargo holding unit. As a result, I looked into Amtrak and found out there was a special train car for handicap accessibility and a 15 percent discount was given to both the caregiver and someone traveling with a disability. A crucial need was an electrical outlet. There was one on the train car that I could use to recharge the battery for the power wheelchair. An attendant on the train would take our meal orders and bring the food to us from the dining car.

I lifted Doug by myself so I knew the trip to Washington, D.C., would be physically challenging for me. I decided to trust Jesus to give me the strength and just enjoy the trip. Doug always wanted to take a trip on Amtrak to the northwestern states after we retired. By God's grace He was allowing us the opportunity to take this all-expense paid trip via Amtrak to Washington, D.C.

We had an appointment in Springfield on March 26 to have preventive maintenance done on the Dodge Ram Van's wheelchair lift. As soon as it was done we planned to head to St. Louis for Doug's appointment the next day. We were delayed when the water pump broke. Thank God it did not happen while I was driving on the interstate to St. Louis! It was after 11 p.m. when we finally arrived in St. Louis and checked into our hotel room.

The medical research team discussed Doug's weight which was 140.4 pounds. Although Doug could still chew and swallow, the staff recommended he have a G-tube soon. I said we would wait until after our trip to Washington, D.C., for the procedure to be done.

We headed to the Springfield ALS Clinic on April 1. It seemed like all we did was go to doctor appointments. The staff recommended several medical procedures for Doug: 1) Get a follow-up chest x-ray from when he had pneumonia, 2) Participate in a sleep study test to see if his breathing is disturbed at night and causes stress on the body, 3) Have a video swallow test and 4) Get a hospital bed. I think the latter was actually to benefit me so instead of me lifting Doug up from a prone position, the hospital bed would raise him up and make it easier for me to lift him into a wheelchair.

Doug rated his quality of life as 7 out of 10. When asked if he noticed any changes in his speech, he replied that sometimes he spoke in a whisper, but for the most part everyone could still understand him. He did not have a saliva issue and did not have any problems swallowing. It just took him a long time to eat when someone fed him. He could not do anything by himself.

While at the clinic I was asked if I would be willing to speak at the MDA'S ALS Awareness Seminar on May 16 in Normal when we returned from Washington, D.C. I was more than happy to and wanted to encourage other ALS patients and their family members.

We celebrated our 27th wedding anniversary on April 3 and ate at our traditional spot. Doug choked while eating so it made me think his swallow test scheduled the following week would be very timely. Inwardly I knew this would be the last anniversary that we would eat at our special location unless Doug was miraculously healed.

I was encouraged by the ALS Association to write a book about our experiences. I was told the ALS Association had never met a family quite like ours and how God divinely intervened in our situation numerous times. Staff members conducting the Knopp Research Study also encouraged me to write our story as they witnessed our faith and struggles.

Doug had a modified Barium swallow function test and a chest x-ray. It was recommended he take small bites of food and chew well before swallowing. If thin liquids caused choking, then we should incorporate nectar or honey to thicken them. Also, I could thicken soups by adding instant mashed potatoes. To help him obtain more calories, he could have an instant breakfast with ice cream.

I was relieved when the need for Doug to have a sleep study test was nixed. I expressed my concern that I would need to be with him throughout the procedure in order to attend to his needs, especially bathroom issues. Instead, Doug was told to have an overnight Finger Pulse Oximeter test like he had before. Again the results were very good.

How to best meet Doug's bathroom needs was constantly a challenge. I carried a urinal everywhere we went so that was an easy solution, but when he needed to have a bowel movement that was a whole other story. We had a portable commode in the living room that I would lift him onto out of his wheelchair. We constantly prayed that no one would come into our home while he was sitting on the commode. We used lots of air freshener! It was a huge blessing when we eventually borrowed a shower chair that also fit over a toilet. It still required lots of lifting on my part, but it was a whole lot easier cleaning up Doug. We also borrowed a sliding shower bench seat that I would lift Doug onto and then slide him across the bathtub when I was giving him a shower.

We received two wonderful blessings that caused me to shout "hallelujah." Illinois State Senator Kyle McCarter's office called and said Sarah won an Illinois General Assembly Scholarship that would pay all of her tuition for the fall, spring and summer 2009-2010 school year. Sarah was extremely excited and determined that if she went to summer school in 2010 then she would be able to graduate in December 2010--a semester early.

In addition to the scholarship, out of the clear blue we received a check in the mail for $3,000 to help with medical bills. Even though we had Medicare and health insurance, we had many out-of-pocket expenses related to the ALS disease. This financial blessing would help pay for these items as well as our monthly insurance premiums and other bills.

Instead of having to drive to St. Louis, Doug's April 24th appointment was actually a telephone interview. He rated his quality of life based on the last two days as 9 out of 10 and basically said he was not having any problems.

Late that afternoon we went to a restaurant and Doug ordered a milkshake with his meal. Suddenly he began having uncontrollable excessive saliva. He could not stop. I quickly boxed up the food and we went home. I knew we would not be able to eat out at restaurants much longer. I prayed Doug would not have any eating issues during our Washington, D.C., trip.

Doug started taking Glycopyrolate for his excessive salivation. We prayed there would not be any side effects from this medication. He continued having intense itching and we tried all kinds of products to provide relief. The medicine Baclofen that he took for the muscle spasms could have an allergic reaction of itching, so Doug was weaned off the medication to see if the itching would subside. It was frustrating for me not being able to take care of Doug's itching. He could not raise his arms to scratch his nose or anywhere on his body anytime he had an itch.

I made the arrangements for our trip to Washington, D.C., and tried to figure out what clothes and equipment to pack. I knew the trip would be a test of my endurance and strength, especially since I had two large suitcases and a carryon bag to manage, let alone Doug in his power wheelchair.

We departed from Springfield's Amtrak Station at 9:55 a.m. on Friday, May 8, and arrived the next day in the afternoon at Union Station in Washington, D.C. It was a very long ride, but we knew it was the best way to travel. Passengers and the train crew were extremely helpful.

While in the nation's capitol, we got to tour the United States Holocaust Memorial Museum. Man's inhumanity to man was well-documented in exhibits throughout the museum. It was emotionally heart wrenching to see everything which reminded us of the Yad Vashem Holocaust History Museum in Israel.

The roll call of the ALS chapters during the opening session of the policy conference was impressive. We saw ALS patients and advocates from across the country. It reinforced the notion that we were not alone. There were many others fighting the same battle as us. Extremely inspiring was the candlelight vigil on the steps of the Carnegie Museum that made many of us weep. It made me pray even more for an ALS cure.

Sessions the next day dealt with research on ALS, educational workshops to discuss policy strategies and clinical breakthroughs for treatment and a cure. We spent Tuesday on Capitol Hill meeting with members of Congress and their staff. I noticed Doug's right hand weakened even more while we tried to maneuver from one congressional office to the next. I ended up operating the joystick. It was a very tight squeeze in some of the elevators. A big complaint I had was the lack of family assisted bathrooms—not a single one on Capitol Hill. Union Stations both in Washington, D.C., and in Chicago were also terrible in providing family assisted bathrooms. I got used to accompanying Doug into the men's restrooms.

The next day we started our journey back home on Amtrak and finally got back to Decatur the evening of May 14. That gave me a day to get unpacked and caught up on everything plus get ready for Saturday's MDA Living for ALS Seminar. We met several families at the seminar struggling with ALS. I prayed I could give them some encouragement. ALS patients, their families and their caregivers all need a boost emotionally and spiritually. Our stories of faith and God's provision blessed those at the seminar and would be a testimony in the future. Once again I was encouraged to write a book. *"They overcame him by the blood of the Lamb and by the word of their testimony; they did not love their lives so much as to shrink from death" (Revelation 12:11).*

Chapter Twelve

II Timothy 4:7 *"I have fought the good fight,
I have finished the race, I have kept the faith."*

It was obvious after our trip to Washington, D.C., that Doug needed a new wheelchair evaluation so that he could operate his chair another way or have the joystick moved to the back of the chair for me to operate.

We went to St. Louis for Doug's May 22 appointment. His breathing test scores were still good, but his weight was down to 136.4 pounds which meant he lost four pounds. It was definitely time for him to get a G-tube. He rated his quality of life at 8 out of 10.

We got home from St. Louis around 5 p.m. only to leave at 7 p.m. to drive to Chicago O'Hare Airport. Sarah was flying back from Central America. I told Doug we would have "noise" in our house with Sarah home. He just smiled and smiled! He was happy his "little girl" would be home for a while. When we got home at 1:30 a.m., several of Sarah's friends were sitting on the curb waiting for our arrival. They had decorated her car with USA items! It was 3 a.m. before we all got to bed.

A friend from New Zealand was in town for his dad's open heart surgery. He stopped by to say hi and to let us know that his family in New Zealand was praying for us.

"Doug is the nicest person. It's hard to understand why God is allowing him to go through this disease," he confided in me.

On May 29 as an out-patient Doug had an endoscopic gastrostomy tube inserted into his stomach. He had to wear a binder over the tube line so it would not get pulled out. The ALS Association had been giving us vouchers for Doug to drink Ensure. The hospital dietician recommended Doug switch to the product Jevity 1.5. He could start with four cans a day and eventually increase to six cans a day.

We received conflicting information about whether Medicare would pay for Jevity 1.5. One person said Doug would have to be homebound in order for Medicare to pay. This meant he could not go to stores or visit people, but he would be allowed to attend church and go to doctor appointments. Another person said Medicare would pay for the Jevity if it was the only nutritional source Doug had and he was not eating anything by mouth.

At the time, Jevity 1.5 cost $2.85 a can so four cans a day would cost $11.40. A year's supply would be $4,161. If he used six cans a day that would cost $17.10 and a year's supply would be $6,241.50. There was no way we could afford that. We decided to keep using Ensure for the time being, and let Doug eat some food by mouth. Praise God, the ALS Association said Doug's voucher for Ensure would be upgraded to Ensure Plus which would be better nutritionally for him. What a blessing!

It was another learning experience to take care of Doug's feeding tube. I have to admit it did not take very long to put the Ensure Plus in the tube as compared to taking an hour to feed Doug a meal. I watched for sales of Ensure Plus because Doug used more of that product every month than what the voucher covered.

On June 1 Doug had an appointment with a speech therapist. His speech was becoming more difficult to understand. Doug tried using a DynaVox EyeMax System. It was calibrated to his eyes and he could "speak" to us using the gaze of his eyes. He could spell words, use the built-in phrases, even sound an alarm if he needed assistance. It cost $17,140. Medicare would pay 80 percent, our insurance company would pay 80 percent of the 20 percent left and then the MDA would pay up to $2,000. A machine was ordered and it would take over a month for its arrival.

Michael had been steadfastly working on his smooth jazz CD "Exceeding Expectations." He wrote all of the songs and did all of the arrangements and production. Before the CD was officially released, he gave us a copy of it. While listening to the song "Sunday Afternoon," Doug started crying. He said he was so proud of Michael and his accomplishments! The project was dedicated to us!

"I would like to say thank you to my mom and dad, who I have dedicated this project to. They have always supported my music career and never missed a concert! I love you both so much!"

On June 27 he released the CD with a phenomenal live concert in Decatur's Lincoln Square Theatre. Prior to the concert he did media interviews. It was a big event in his life and I am so glad his dad was there to share in it. Eventually his CD was ranked 41 on the U.S. jazz charts.

We did not have to travel to St. Louis on June 19 but instead Doug had a phone interview regarding the Knopp Study. When asked how he was feeling in the last two days taking into consideration his physical, social, spiritual, financial and emotional state, Doug replied it was 8 out of 10.

"With my wife helping me, it makes for good quality of life," Doug explained.

He said his voice was sometimes a whisper and every now and then he had some excessive saliva. He had not had any choking episodes and was not drooling.

To keep track of Doug's weight on a weekly basis, we made arrangements with a dietician at a local hospital to weigh Doug on the laundry scale. He stayed in his power wheelchair, and we subtracted the weight of the chair to see how much he weighed.

Doug turned 60 on July 7 and I decided to do a big celebration on July 11. We had 50 family members and friends come from several states to wish him a happy birthday. It was a great time and he thoroughly enjoyed visiting with everyone.

When we stayed at the Parkway Hotel in St. Louis, we always reserved a handicap accessible room and bathroom. The hotel's roll-in shower was very convenient so I got bids for remodeling our bathroom with that feature, but the price tag ranged from $4,700 to $8,600. That was too expensive for us. In addition, if the bathtub was taken out, then there would not be one in the house. We decided to forego the remodeling and do the best we could with what we had.

On Doug's July 17 appointment in St. Louis he had a hard time giving blood. It took four different nurses to finally "stick" him and get results. They explained it is not uncommon for ALS patients to have a hard time giving blood because the muscles quit working. Doug was my hero for all that he was doing for ALS research, especially when one considered he never took medicine or went to doctors for the 31 years he was healthy and worked as a bus driver.

During this visit, Doug rated his quality of life as 7 out of 10. He admitted that oftentimes his speech was difficult for people to understand so he had to repeat himself. Also, he noticed a slight increase in his saliva. His weight was 138.2 pounds and he was averaging three cans of Ensure Plus a day plus still eating solid food.

A few days later Doug had some "goop" and a little blood around the G-tube port. The hospital wound nurse said it was a common problem called hyper granulation.

"His skin looks wonderful! I'm impressed. You've done good taking care of the tube and the skin around it," she commented.

It was comforting to hear her remarks. Being a caregiver can be a lonely job and at times discouraging. I admired those in the nursing profession. I never wanted to be a nurse, but between my mom's medical needs and Doug's, I had done a lot of nursing care.

We continued trying different pieces of equipment—some were helpful and some were not. A hydraulic lift to help me lift

Doug was just too big. Transfer boards were awkward to use. Doug no longer used the lift chair in our living room because he was in his power wheelchair all day long. We borrowed a Duraglide shower chair, but it was too high up for Michael and me to lift Doug onto. It was more work than just using the bench seat that slid over the tub. We finally got the mount installed on Doug's chair for his DynaVox EyeMax System and he practiced using the machine.

We made another trip to St. Louis for Doug's August 14 appointment. I signed consent forms for Doug to continue to be in the Knopp Study for another two years, but he questioned if he would last that long.

His weight was down to 136 pounds, but he still rated his quality of life as 8 out of 10.

"It's been pretty good the last two days," he remarked.

When we went into the cafeteria to eat lunch, I noticed a plaque with the scripture verse Jeremiah 17:14, *"Heal me, O Lord, and I will be healed."*

"Scratch me, O wife, and I will be scratched," was Doug's quick reply because he continually had itches. We both had a good laugh!

Our bedroom furniture had to be rearranged to accommodate Doug's hospital bed. Our bed was put in Sarah's bedroom and I bought a twin bed for myself. It was different not sleeping with Doug anymore, but at least I could keep him at home and be near him without putting him in a nursing home.

Some days were tougher than others, and I came to the conclusion that I hated the disease of ALS with a passion. I hated how it affected the patient and his family. At times both Doug and I were discouraged. He could hardly operate his power wheelchair anymore—that was his last bastion of independence. Bathroom issues and accidents were happening more frequently. We did not see any signs of healing; rather, there was more advancement of the disease even though we had people around the world praying for us. There were times when he indicated he just wanted to die and go to heaven.

Doug's itching became intense and we wondered if it was a side effect from the Knopp experimental drug. The staff at Washington University School of Medicine finally decided to let Doug "take a holiday" from the Knopp medicine and see if it was the source of the itching. If there was not any change, then he would possibly resume taking the medication at our next St. Louis visit.

The MDA asked us to participate in the TELU event in Champaign. People were put "in jail" to raise money for the Jerry Lewis Telethon scheduled for Labor Day weekend. We were extremely appreciative of everything the MDA did for us and gladly participated in the event. We were filmed with individuals presenting us checks for the MDA. Several people told us they saw those filmed segments during the actual telethon. Because there was a drop in donations, the MDA could no longer offer an equipment allowance as it had in the past. My heart went out to families who ended up absorbing more of these costs.

A monthly ALS Support Group started in Springfield September 8 so we drove over for the meeting. We met several individuals including Robert Floyd, who was 37-years-old with ALS. He was very fearful of the disease and about dying. His wife Andrea was very angry, and honestly, she had every right to be. I do not know of anyone who is happy to have ALS. They had not been married very long and were facing difficult times. We shared about God's grace and the blessings He had provided for us. After the meeting, Doug and I had a tremendous burden for this couple and prayed for them often. In God's timing He had a beautiful plan unfolding with our association with them.

When Doug's monthly Social Security Disability check arrived, it did not take long for me to spend it while paying bills. We really needed a financial breakthrough because we had some additional expenses. In the mail someone unexpectantly sent us a check for $300. What timing from God! I cried and so did Doug!

At Doug's September 10 appointment in St. Louis, he rated his quality of life as 6 out of 10, the lowest yet. I explained to the research nurse that Doug experienced several recent adverse events including a terrible choking incident, blood in his stool, the inability to move his hand to operate his wheelchair, a constant runny nose, severe itching and more excess saliva and drooling. He also experienced pain in his neck, shoulder and hip.

Doug's blood work from that visit revealed his triglycerides had gotten higher. It was recommended Doug get started on Jevity because it contains less sugar than Ensure Plus.

Our new health insurance company would not pay for any of the Jevity. In fact it would not pay for a lot of Doug's needs so we ended up paying for them ourselves. Medicare would pay for 80 percent of the Jevity and a medical supply company said it would take care of the rest of it on their end. We were extremely grateful for their generosity, but frustrated with this new insurance company.

Doug actually gained two pounds from his previous weigh-in at the hospital laundry scale. The dietician said 139.4 was a good weight, but if he got up to 145 pounds, then that would be too much for me to lift.

"It's fat and not muscles," she reminded me of Doug's weight.

Doug started using the cough assist machine on a daily basis. He had trouble swallowing pills so I crushed them and put them in his feeding tube. Not only was the feeding tube essential for getting nutritional drinks, but it was also a great avenue for him to ingest his medicine. Eventually he took as many as seven different medicines a day.

Waiting for equipment approval from Medicare was a nightmare. We were still awaiting approval for Doug to receive switches so he could operate his power wheelchair with his knees. It would then take another month or more to receive the equipment after the approval. Walking alongside Doug's wheelchair and trying to operate it was very difficult for me, especially when going up wheelchair ramps. There was not enough room for me to walk side-by-side. The wheelchair specialist asked if we wanted him to move the joystick to the back of the chair for easier operation by me.

I asked Doug what he thought and he replied, "It wouldn't bother me." It was time for me to assume all of the responsibility for operating the chair.

We received the October 2009 issue of the Levitt Letter from Zola Levitt Ministries and were absolutely stunned to see our family picture and a letter that I had written to Dr. Jeffrey Seif about Doug's ALS. God had already given us a national spotlight with the disease and now we were having an international spotlight with this ministry. Dr. Seif remembered us from the 2007 Israel trip and asked their readers to remember us in prayer.

I was notified by the ALS Association St. Louis Regional Chapter that November was National Caregiver Month and I was selected by their organization as a National Caregiver. I remarked that all caregivers are worthy and deserving of being honored as a national caregiver.

"I've learned to be a servant," I commented.

Because I was lifting Doug several times a day by myself, I purchased a back brace so I would have additional support. The last thing we needed was for me to get hurt.

Doug could not be left alone, so I was grateful when Ted Summers from church came over nearly every Wednesday to spend time with Doug. Oftentimes he fed him lunch. Our CHELP (Community Home Environmental Learning Project) worker, who was hired with the respite grant, many times went beyond the call of duty to assist us. My "gas angel" not only helped pay for gas, but she made a cape for Doug. I could not get his arms in the sleeves of a coat. The weather was getting colder and I needed to keep Doug warm when we went out. She not only made a cape, but she also made a "mink" blanket and fixed a rain poncho for him. Now I could take him outside in adverse weather conditions.

We borrowed an alternating air pressure pad overlay for Doug's hospital bed. His bony left shoulder blade had redness from when he slept at night. The overlay was similar to an air mattress, but had a motor that allowed the air pressure to alternate. This provided more comfortable accomodations.

Doug had a telephone call interview on October 12 from Washington University Medical Research Center. He rated his quality of life as 5 out of 10, the lowest number yet.

I solicited donations for our Szach Pack Team for the October 17 Springfield ALS Walk. I was grateful for Doug's cape and blanket because it was very cold that day. For some reason Doug's wheelchair would not go fast, so we ended up not doing the three mile walk. Instead, we went back inside the building. It was probably a wise idea to get Doug out of the cold air since he had pneumonia earlier in the year.

Our ALS Patient Services Coordinator's visit on October 21 was a reality check for me. She asked me if we had in writing what we wanted done medically if Doug went into respiratory arrest and I had to call 911. I told her I had power of attorney including the ability to make medical decisions. She said that was good. Doug and I both agreed he did not want long-term mechanical ventilation. Everyone in our family needed to be aware of that decision. She indicated in most ALS cases, the patients do not want a ventilator because of the way the disease progresses.

She recommended Doug get a suction machine because of his excessive saliva and also a bi-pap machine because his breathing scores were low—less than 50 percent now. It was her next suggestion that threw me for a loop! She encouraged us to enroll Doug in hospice care for a six-month period. She emphasized that it was not because Doug was dying, but because his ALS was progressing and hospice would provide several services that he needed. A hospice nurse would come twice a week to check Doug's vitals and see if he needed anything. If we had a medical question, we could talk to her about it.

When I questioned our ALS Patient Services Coordinator

how long she thought Doug would live, he promptly piped in "if I make it to December 27."

I asked him what he meant by that. He proceeded to tell us that sometime during the night of September 27 while lying in bed the words "you have three months to live" flashed before him on the wall. I was in shock! Why didn't he tell me this before?

"I guess I didn't really need to tell you," he commented.

I was dumbfounded! If that was true then he only had a little over two months to live. It was as though the air was sucked right out of me. I really cannot explain it, but at that moment my faith to believe Doug could be healed was suddenly gone. God had another plan. I did not want to worry anyone, especially Sarah who was already stressed with college, so I decided not to tell anyone. I actually ended up confiding in one person, but she was not close by.

We agreed to have Doug evaluated for hospice care. When asked what his biggest fear or concerns were, he replied, "I'm ready to go (to heaven) whenever."

If he was accepted into hospice, we would not be allowed to call 911 if he fell or if something serious happened. Instead, we had to call the hospice organization. I was amazed to learn that hospice would pay for everything. We had experienced lots of out-of-pocket expenses especially co-pay on medicines when dealing with ALS. Hospice would even pay for the gauze and tape that I used for Doug's feeding tube.

October 26 was another milestone with Doug's ALS. He was approved for hospice and I signed the papers. On that same day he lost his neck muscles and what little leg muscles he had left. He could no longer hold his head up on his own and he could no longer help me with his legs when I transferred him from one piece of equipment to another. His body went limp which made him seem like dead weight. From now on I needed Michael's help to lift his dad. Hospice ordered a special neck collar and a suction machine which became a life safer. Doug was having huge saliva issues and I was afraid he would choke. Thankfully the machine was delivered the next day. It was getting harder and harder to leave the house.

The insurance company that sent Doug the short-term medical disability payments when he was first diagnosed with ALS wrote me a letter stating that if Doug was approved, he was eligible for a $25,000 life insurance policy. There were lots of insurance papers for me to fill out and the ALS doctor had to verify Doug's continued disability.

Michael was gone the evening of November 1 and it was getting late. I needed to get Doug ready for bed and decided to lift Doug by myself out of his power wheelchair and put him on the stair lift. I should have known better. His legs buckled, and he fell to the floor. I screamed for my mom to come but the two of us could not pick him up. I called my brother Kirk who came immediately. Doug was on his knees and obviously in pain. Kirk got his legs stretched out and helped him sit up. He lifted him onto the stair lift and then helped me get him into the manual wheelchair. We wheeled him into the bedroom and then lifted him onto the bed. While getting him undressed, I noticed a few drops of blood on his sweater. We surmised he must have bit his cheek when he fell. Doug could not get to sleep and around 12:10 a.m. he let me know he needed some pain medicine.

A physical therapist from hospice came and recommended several exercises to keep Doug's muscles working, some that should be done every hour. To me it was ridiculous spending the time doing them—he hardly had any muscles left that even worked! Besides, I was sometimes spending an hour at a time just suctioning Doug and then using the cough assist machine.

He had not been able to wear his wedding band for over a year because of the swelling in his hands. When he entered the hospice program, I decided to wear his ring on my thumb. It was too big for the rest of my fingers. It reminded me of the time in 1976 when Doug proposed to me. I wore my engagement ring on my thumb until it was sized smaller.

When I got out of the shower on the morning of November 4, I noticed Doug's wedding band was missing. I calmly prayed and asked God to help me find it. Somehow I knew it was going to be found. I looked in the bedroom, living room, washing machine, etc., but it was nowhere to be found. I kept praying but did not tell anyone. I prayed that the hidden things would be revealed. I looked in the handicap van, but did not see it. I prayed that God would help me find it before we left at 10 a.m. for St. Louis.

I decided that when I found it, I would no longer wear it on my thumb because I did not want to lose it again. Instead, I would put it on a chain and wear it around my neck. I went back out to the van to look. While sitting on the driver's side and searching the inside of the van, the thought occurred to me that maybe when I got home from the pharmacy the previous evening, perhaps I flung it off when I reached into my pocket. Nearly every day I was going to the pharmacy to get a new medication or get an old one refilled for Doug. I decided to open the van door and as I glanced on the ground, there was the ring in the grass. It was a miracle! Nothing is impossible for God! Only by God's grace did I see the ring on the grass at the edge of the concrete driveway. I wanted to wear Doug's ring as a reminder of his love for me and my love for him. We made a covenant relationship on April 3, 1982, and like the ring, our love for each other was unbroken.

Doug's visit in St. Louis was terrible. For a second time he rated his quality of life as 5 out of 10, and his EKG results were abnormal. When the physical therapist tried to administer the breathing test, Doug had major problems with mucus secretions. The breathing test was skipped. It made me wonder if we would be able to come back for any more appointments.

When Doug went on hospice, we talked about making an appointment with a funeral home to make some pre-arrangements. The President/Director of Graceland/Fairlawn Funeral Home and Cemeteries came to our home to help us start making arrangements. I felt God leading me to pre-pay for the funeral and the only way I could do that was if I tapped into

Doug's IRA. I was actually too young to take any money out, but because I had power of attorney I could. In the back of my mind I knew I would need some money to live on if Doug died, and I needed money for Sarah's next semester of college. Once Doug died, his Social Security Disability payments would cease. I would not have any income. The only thing I was eligible to receive was a one-time $255 death benefit from Social Security. I was 55 years old and too young to receive anything else.

We were invited by the ALS Association St. Louis Regional Chapter to attend the ALS Holiday and Awards Dinner. I wanted to go but I knew with Doug's deteriorating condition it would be an extremely difficult trip. We found out that we were selected for the Outstanding Support in Advocacy & Awareness Award for 2009. It was an awesome recognition! Because we could not attend in person, the award was mailed to us.

Our hospice nurse was wonderful in advising us about various situations that confronted us. Doug was having more bathroom accidents and I was at my wits end. She suggested Doug wear an external catheter with a leg bag. Even then he had accidents if the catheter was not on correctly. I constantly had to have help lifting him so I could change him and get him cleaned up. It was uncanny how many times someone stopped by our house just as I needed assistance lifting Doug. What was amazing was how Doug always had a good attitude about everything and never complained.

Sarah came home for Thanksgiving break on Monday night. Doug and I decided that North Fork Cemetery was where he would be buried. My dad was buried there. When I was a kid, I rode my bicycle in that cemetery. I took Sarah with me on Tuesday to pick out and buy two burial plots—one for Doug and one for me. Amazingly, we ended up getting plots very near my dad's. It was a very emotional day and one that had Sarah and me crying often, but it needed to be done.

We had a wonderful Thanksgiving Day spent with family and were blessed with two Thanksgiving baskets. Doug's sister and family came for our annual Thanksgiving dinner. I am sure it was hard for her to see her brother suffering with ALS, especially after their mom and aunt had died of the disease. We asked her husband to be a pallbearer and he promptly agreed. We had a family picture taken with them and used it in our Christmas card.

Later that evening Doug and I gave Michael and Sarah Thanksgiving cards. Doug painstakingly dictated something specifically for each of them. The verse inside Michael's card stated "It's natural at Thanksgiving to express what's always true—It really means a lot to have a special son like you." Doug then dictated to me, "Michael, when you were born, God put you on the path of greatness and I have had the opportunity to watch your life bloom. Thanks for taking care of me. I love you! Keep on serving and trusting the Lord. Love, Dad"

The outside of Sarah's card said "For a dear daughter" and the verse inside said, "You're a wonderful daughter—that's certainly true—And so many nice things could be said about you…But words only tell you a very small part of how special you are and how close to the heart!" Doug dictated these words to her, "Sarah, the three stanzas of this card pretty well cover anything that I might have said by myself. Keep on seeking the Lord and put Him first in all you do. I love you! Love, Dad"

Doug started taking a low dosage of morphine to help him with his pain and with his breathing. He was having major problems with excessive saliva, so the hospice nurse told us about Transderm patches that he could wear behind his ears. Doug was willing to try anything and I wanted to make him as comfortable as possible.

I really wanted Michael and Sarah to meet the medical staff at Washington University Medical Research Center for Doug's December 11 appointment and see what their dad's visit entailed each time he went there. Sarah finished her last exam for the semester at Northern Illinois University around 7:30 p.m. on December 10 and then drove to Decatur. We awaited her arrival and then left for St. Louis around 11 p.m. We were going to have some family time, even though it was not under the best circumstances.

Doug's weight was 142.8 pounds and his vital signs were good. This visit was going to be a long one because it required 12 vials of blood to be drawn from Doug over the course of the day. Michael and Sarah were amazed at what their dad endured for research.

We made arrangements to spend a second night in the hotel. Our wonderful friends Mark and Evvy Bowman met us in the lobby of the hotel and came up to our room. We reminisced about our friendship over the years. Evvy later remarked how Doug still maintained his sense of humor despite his condition. Mark had already agreed to be one of Doug's pallbearers. Michael and Sarah had fun joining two of their cousins for supper in the hotel's adjacent restaurant. Everyone had a great time! I think we all knew it would be our last trip to St. Louis for the Knopp Study.

Our hospice social worker forewarned me about anticipatory grief and that sometimes we cry and grieve before our loved one dies. For some people it actually shortens the grieving process. We "anticipate" what is going to happen. That happened to Michael who said he just cried and cried after he got to church Sunday morning following our St. Louis visit. I had already had several moments of wondering what was going to happen after Doug died. What would it be like living without him? Who would I talk to? I would need to be both mom and "dad" for the kids. Doug would not be there for important events in their lives. How would I survive financially without any income from him? How could I make decisions without his input?

The hospice nurse came the next day and said Doug's blood pressure was higher than usual and he had more upper airway congestion. In addition he had shortness of breath, but he told us he did not feel anxious. He had pain in his right leg. She recommended Doug be given liquid morphine every couple of hours to help with the shortness of breath.

During her visits with us, she kept us informed about Robert Floyd's ALS progression. She was also his hospice nurse and spent a lot of time driving back and forth from his home in Jacksonville to our home in Decatur, taking care of both men. Both Andrea and I had given her permission to share information.

On the afternoon of December 19, I asked Doug if he thought he was dying. He looked at me kind of funny and said no. Late that night, everything changed and he told me he was dying. The kids started crying. Michael asked if each of them could spend some time alone with their dad. I said sure. We stayed up until 4 a.m. and then Doug finally went to sleep. I decided to share with the kids Doug's vision of the words "You have three months to live" and how one month of that time had gone by before Doug told me. They were shocked! I told them how merciful God was to me to start preparing for the inevitable earthly departure of their dad. I explained to them that was why I prepaid for Doug's funeral and planned some of his service. They finally understood my motivation.

On December 22 the same wonderful Christian lady, who had talked to me in the grocery store a year earlier and asked me "where is God in all of this," called and said she had something for me. I had not talked to her since our encounter. She said her father had passed away in April, and she recently received some of her inheritance.

"I knew there were two things I was supposed to do. One was pay my pledge to WBGL Christian Radio Station and the second was to bless you. I just want you to know that your emails have touched me," she remarked.

From time to time I wrote a mass email keeping people informed of what was happening with Doug. One of his high school classmates posted my emails on Facebook so fellow classmates could be kept informed about Doug's condition. Several wrote Doug to let him know they were praying for him, and some mentioned they had become born again Christians—just thrilling Doug to no end!

I was absolutely amazed when the woman pulled out

her checkbook and wrote me a check for $500. Wow! What a blessing! God knew I would need that money in the days ahead. She proceeded to tell me about a Caregiver's Bible. I decided to order one as a Christmas gift for Andrea and sent Robert the Bible on CDs.

That same day we received a letter from the life insurance company informing us that Doug had been approved for the $25,000 life insurance policy. The timing could not have been more perfect! It was a bonus gift from God, letting me know He would take care of me financially.

Late that night Doug had difficulty breathing and turned purple. He needed suctioning and then seemed to get better. Since we were unable to attend our church's Candlelight Communion Service, we did a family communion around midnight. My brother Kirk brought to our home the church's offering plate with the promise scripture verses so we each selected one for the coming year. It was amazing how each verse we drew out was a "rhema" word from God.

Michael's verse was Haggai 2:9. *"'The glory of this present house will be greater than the glory of the former house,' says the Lord Almighty. 'And in this place I will grant peace,' declares the Lord Almighty."*

Sarah's verse was Psalm 30:5. *"For His anger lasts only a moment, but His favor lasts a lifetime; weeping may remain for a night, but rejoicing comes in the morning."*

Doug's verse was Proverbs 19:17. *"He who is kind to the poor lends to the Lord, and He will reward him for what he has done."*

My verse was Jeremiah 17:7. *"But blessed is the man who trusts in the Lord, whose confidence is in Him."*

Michael got out some old family videos, and we all had a good time watching them and laughing. About 1:30 a.m. we got Doug to bed. He was not there very long before he had difficulty breathing. He was dying again.

"Let me go!" he said over and over again.

I called the kids to quickly come upstairs. Michael thought

for sure his dad was going home to the Lord because the coloring was leaving his face. I told Michael we needed to get Doug out of the bed and back into his power wheelchair. I decided Doug could no longer sleep in his bed but would need to stay in his power wheelchair in the living room. I would sleep on the couch to be near him.

To be honest, this was not a good time for Doug to die. All of my family would be gathering at our home in two days on Christmas Eve for a gift exchange and then I had a big dinner to fix for family on Christmas Day. My brother Kirk, who would officiate at Doug's funeral, was going to Mexico on a mission's trip with all of his family. They were leaving at midnight on Christmas Day and would not return until the evening of January 2. My brother Kim, who lived in Montana, was going to be a pallbearer but he was anxiously awaiting the birth of his granddaughter. By God's grace, Doug rallied and we had a wonderful Christmas Eve and Christmas Day.

A couple of days after Christmas, Sarah asked me when I thought her dad would die. She was worried about classes starting for her spring semester and how everything would work out. I did not know what to tell her but assured her God had everything under control. I was most concerned about Sarah and how her dad's death would affect her.

Kim called to let us know that baby Leah was born December 29. The timing was perfect! I was a great aunt and Doug was pleased to be a great uncle. He continued to hang in there. Several times during the nights of the 29th and 30th he woke me up, trying to get my attention. He tried to talk, but was unable to speak. He kept looking up to the ceiling, indicating there was something up there, but I did not see anything. I wondered if it might have been angels.

On New Year's Eve in the morning, I told Doug, "Honey, you've lived through 2009 and it looks like you will live to see 2010." He just smiled.

We made plans to have our friends Craig and Kathy Patient spend the evening with us and usher in the New Year as they had done previously. Sarah left in the afternoon to work in banqueting at a hotel's annual New Year's Eve bash. Everything seemed to be going okay when all of a sudden Doug started having difficulties breathing. He kept telling me, "Help me. Help me." I honestly did not know what to do but pray. Michael asked him if he should get Sarah home because he was dying and he nodded yes. Craig and Kathy left and Sarah came in the door at 8:45 p.m. Once again we said our good-byes only this time it was permanent. Within 30 minutes Doug was ushered into heaven. I firmly believe he was escorted by the angels he tried to tell me about. I called my neighbor, who was a nurse, and she quickly came over, confirming his death.

I called hospice. The person scheduled to be on duty if someone died that night was the chaplain who lived in Jacksonville. He was notified and then drove 70 miles to our home, arriving around 11 p.m. He called the coroner's office and the funeral home. Finally, at 11:50 p.m. a deputy coroner arrived. As soon as she entered our home she made the comment, "The official time of death is not until I arrive." All I could think was if she had arrived 10 minutes later, she would have said Doug's official time of death was in 2010. That would have been crazy for my family because we knew Doug actually went home to Jesus at 9:15 p.m. on December 31, 2009.

"Precious in the sight of the Lord is the death of His saints" *(Psalm 116:15).*

Chapter Thirteen

II Timothy 4:8a *"Now there is in store for me the crown of righteousness."*

It almost seemed providential for Doug to die the last day of the year. God decided he had suffered enough, and I would literally start 2010 as a new year in my life. Michael, Sarah and I spent part of New Year's Day making all of the final funeral arrangements. Over and over again we thanked God for directing me a few weeks earlier to buy a burial plot at North Fork Cemetery, especially since we were now dealing with a holiday weekend. We decided to have the visitation on Sunday evening, January 3, and the funeral on Monday. This would give time for Kirk and his family to get back from the mission trip and for Kim to fly from Montana.

I spent the rest of New Year's Day writing Doug's obituary, writing a mass email about the news of Doug's death, composing my eulogy and getting photos ready for a DVD memorial tribute. Michael's jazz song "Sunday Afternoon" would be played as background music during the DVD tribute. The next day Sarah and I went to the funeral home with the photos and set up a display of Doug's trumpet, shofar, bus awards, ALS award, a digital frame of photos and many other meaningful mementoes. I wanted Doug's visitation and funeral to be a witness to the community about his life and faith in Jesus.

I held up very well emotionally during the visitation until the bus drivers came in, wearing their uniforms. They gathered together in a semi-circle around the casket and me and saluted their comrade. It was very touching! They were grieving the loss of their special friend and co-worker. Over and over again the drivers thanked me for having the visitation on a Sunday night because that was the only night of the week the city buses did not run and they could come together as a group. It would be impossible for them to get time off the next day to attend the funeral. One of their last honors to Doug was making arrangements to have the bus trolley be in the funeral procession from the funeral home to the cemetery.

I had one other emotional moment during the visitation when one of Doug's cousins made the comment that Doug's right thumb was now whole and he was walking on the streets of gold, unassisted. No more power wheelchair!

During the funeral, I was very proud of Michael and Sarah for the stories of tribute they shared honoring their dad. The 1960's song "Oh Happy Day" was played and then Michael played on the piano a medley of songs that Doug had also requested including "I'll Fly Away" and "Soon and Very Soon (We Are Going to See The King)." Michael encouraged the audience to join in singing the last song. It was quite a celebration!

I shared that Doug has a new address. I believed with all my heart that he received numerous jewels in his crown when he got to heaven because of his servant's attitude and for his generosity in helping others. I am sure Kirk began to wonder if he would ever get to speak, but he finally did and his remarks were uplifting. Everything was a powerful tribute to a humble man who drove a city bus, who loved the Lord and often chose to be behind the scenes. He touched so many lives! Several people came up to me afterwards and said they had never been to a funeral like Doug's!

The funeral director later told me that Doug's visitation and funeral had the distinction of several firsts for his funeral home: it was the largest visitation ever for anyone his age (easily 500 to 600 and many people left when they saw the line); it was the first time there was such a lively celebration with people singing and clapping, and in the overflow room people were dancing (usually funerals are somber and quiet); it was the longest funeral service ever recorded there and it was the first time anyone used a digital frame. An estimated 220 people were at the funeral which was a tremendous number because not that many go to funerals any more—most people just go to the visitation. Several individuals told me they could not come to the visitation or funeral because of the weather—it was bitterly cold and there was snow on the ground. Others said they would have come but were still gone for the holidays.

It was an adjustment getting used to the new found freedom I had. No longer did I have to find someone to stay with Doug if I needed to leave. No longer did I have to hurry home if I went somewhere. I had been going on ".fumes" for sleep. It was strange not getting up in the middle of the night and taking care of Doug's needs.

Dealing with financial matters was extremely time-consuming. It was incredible the number of places that had to have a death certificate or a copy of one when taking Doug's name off of accounts. Just when I thought I was done, something else would come up.

Anyone who experiences grief will find comfort and consolation in different places. For me it was a contemporary Christian artist's song that dealt with the various scenarios in people's lives. I identified with several of them and played the song over and over again because it ministered to me. I had the local Christian bookstore make several copies of that song, which I distributed to women going through difficult situations or who were widows like me. Just using the term widow seemed like a foreign word. In my mind, I was too young to be a widow.

Someone told me about a wonderful web site called www.griefshare.org where a person can sign up for 365 daily emails to help go through the grieving process. It was a great source of comfort to receive an email every day that put into words what I was feeling.

I received word that Robert Floyd wanted to see someone to be assured of being saved and forgiven. Could it be that Doug's illness and death from ALS would bring people into God's kingdom? Doug and I had prayed often that Robert would not die before accepting Jesus Christ as his Savior and Lord.

I finally had some free time about a week after Doug's funeral and drove to Jacksonville. When I arrived at Robert and Andrea's residence, I asked Andrea if I could highlight some scripture verses in the Caregiver's Bible I sent her for Christmas. She gave me permission and said I could also highlight verses in an old Bible that belonged to Robert. After sharing with them about salvation, I had the privilege and the honor of praying with both of them and their caregiver to accept Jesus Christ as their Savior and Lord. It was an awesome moment! In Hebrews 12:1 the apostle Paul writes that we are surrounded by a great cloud of witnesses. I couldn't help but think that Doug was watching this momentous occasion.

The hospice staff later thanked me over and over again for being a source of inspiration and encouragement to this couple. They also encouraged me to write a book.

A couple of weeks later I received an email from Andrea. Robert was having dreams where he saw doors that were closed. He kept trying to find one that would open. Finally, he succeeded in opening a door. He walked into a room that was filled with bright light and noticed people walking around with crowns on their heads.

"Tell Viki that she would be shocked at how big Doug's crown was because of all the people he affected while he was on earth," he told his wife.

I was overwhelmed with such a profound insight into heaven! It greatly encouraged me as well as comforted me. Later I asked Andrea if she knew we get crowns when we go to heaven.

"No, I didn't know that."

I then asked her if she thought her husband knew about the crowns.

"Oh, I'm sure he didn't know that."

A week later I went back to visit them. Robert could hardly talk, but he wanted me to know two more details about his dream—the crowns were golden and there were jewels in them. How amazing! At Doug's funeral I talked about jewels in his crown. I proceeded to write several scripture verses for Andrea about crowns.

My visits with them confirmed my need to write a book about my journey of faith and let others know that heaven is a place where God rewards His children. According to Revelation 21:3, God will spend time with each person who goes to heaven. It will be an awesome place where Christians can continue relationships with the people they love. There will not be any death in heaven and no more separation.

I designed Doug's tombstone to be a witness for anyone who might visit the North Fork Cemetery. Etched on the front left corner was a trumpet and on the right corner a shofar. Centered in the top middle was the scripture verse found in Joel 2:1 and 15, *"Blow the trumpet in Zion."* The name SCHERER was in the middle of the stone. Doug's name was on the left and mine on the right. In between were wedding rings with our wedding date of April 3, 1982 and the word SHALOM under the date. On the backside was the name SCHERER and the scripture verse, *"For to me, to live is Christ and to die is gain" (Philippians 1:21).*

I must admit, the first time I went to the cemetery to see the tombstone it was pretty overwhelming, but a necessary part of the grieving process. It was finality. As a Christian, I knew Doug was not there anyway. He was walking around heaven with a golden crown on his head!

I gave back to the ALS Association lots of medical equipment that we borrowed and donated to it Doug's DynaVox EyeMax System. I wanted another ALS patient to benefit from that wonderful communication device. I donated Doug's power wheelchair to the Muscular Dystrophy Association and hoped it would provide great mobility for someone with a neuromuscular disease.

I did not cry about the return of any equipment until a medical supply company came to get the cough assist machine, the suction machine and lastly Doug's hospital bed. There was a huge void in the bedroom with the absence of the bed. It was another closure in my life as a caregiver for my wonderful husband.

I had several ALS families in Illinois and Missouri contact me about the stair lifts. It was extremely difficult trying to determine who got them. I decided right then that I wished I was a philanthropist who could buy equipment for ALS families because I knew exactly where they were coming from. They wanted to provide the best quality care for their loved ones suffering with ALS.

Former First Lady of the United States Rosalynn Carter once said, "There are only four kinds of people in the world—those who have been caregivers, those who are currently caregivers, those who will be caregivers and those who will need caregivers." I believe her statement pretty much covers all of us.

On May 15 I received a phone call from the hospice nurse. "Doug greeted Robert 45 minutes ago (1:15 p.m.)." Although he suffered terribly with ALS, Robert knew he was going to heaven and he could not wait to see Doug. There were tears in many eyes when I shared during Robert's Memorial Service the testimony of his salvation and his glimpse into heaven.

I got back into substitute teaching but was concerned what I would do for income over the summer. God works in mysterious ways and orchestrated a plan that would benefit me and our church.

In 1986 the House of Prayer, pastored by my dad Rev. Jerry Henneberry, and Bethel Tabernacle, pastored by Rev. Don Etnier, merged to form Harvest Christian Center. In January of 2010 my brother Kirk was praying about Harvest and for the first time he felt released by God from the neighborhood where our church was located. Unbeknown to us and at the same time, Pastor Norm Etnier was praying about retiring from Christian

Fellowship. Kirk liked the visible location of that building so Norm and Kirk decided to merge their congregations and the property was signed over to Harvest. Who would ever dream 24 years after Norm's dad and my dad formed Harvest Christian Center that the two sons would get the same opportunity? With the new growing church, I got hired as the administrative assistant! God's timing was perfect!

In the year that follows a loved one's death, there are many firsts to experience especially if the person was a spouse—first Valentine's Day without him, first wedding anniversary, first birthday, first Christmas and other holidays without his presence.

It is also tough when there are major events in your children's lives like marriage and college graduation. Doug's absence was felt when Michael married Quinishai Cobb on November 20, 2010, and when Sarah graduated from Northern Illinois University on December 12, 2010. She was allowed 10 tickets to the graduation ceremony and saved one for her dad so "he would have a seat to watch her graduate."

Each person goes through grief differently and at different paces. It is important not to stay in the past but to move forward and realize that God loves me more than I will ever know. He has a plan and a purpose for my life and will be with me as I continue my journey of faith. Where there is faith, He is with you. *"The only thing that counts is faith expressing itself through love" (Galatians 5:6).*

Epilogue

I would be remiss if I did not present the opportunity for you to become a born again believer. Jesus said in John 3:3, *"I tell you the truth, no one can see the kingdom of God unless he is born again."* Jesus continued His discourse about salvation later in chapter three with the well-known verses of 3:16-17. *"For God so loved the world that He gave His only begotten Son, that whoever believes in Him should not perish but have everlasting life. For God did not send His Son into the world to condemn the world, but that the world through Him might be saved" (NKJV ™).*

You may argue there are many roads that lead to eternity spent in heaven, but Jesus said in John 14:6, *"I am the way and the truth, and the life. No one comes to the Father except through Me."* In Acts 4:12 while addressing the Sanhedrin, the Apostle Peter stated, *"Salvation is found in no one else, for there is no other name under heaven given to men by which we must be saved."*

Perhaps you are under the assumption that you can "earn" your way to heaven by doing good works. You might be the best caregiver in the world or the most loving individual who gives his time and money to charity, but your good deeds will not save you and provide you an entrance into heaven. The Apostle Paul wrote in Ephesians 2:8-9, *"For by grace you have been saved through faith, and that not of yourselves; it is the gift of God, not of works, lest anyone should boast" (NKJV ™).*

None of us knows the day or the hour when we will be called into eternity. There are no guarantees any of us will be alive tomorrow. Besides, we are just passing through this world. ALS is actually a rare disease, but there are many other diseases that can inflict a person unexpectedly. We are living in crazy times where world disasters and calamaties can happen instantly or where random acts of violence can occur at any location. Hebrews 9:27 states, *"It is appointed for men to die once, but after this the judgment" (NKJV ™).* Maybe you are like Doug and you know you only have a short time to live. That is all the more reason to get your life right with the Lord. *"Today, if you hear His voice, do not harden your hearts" (Hebrews 4:7).*

Jesus said in Mark 8:35-36, *"For whoever wants to save his life will lose it, but whoever loses his life for Me and for the gospel will save it. What good is it for a man to gain the whole world, yet forfeit his soul?"*

In the parable of the rich fool found in Luke 12:16-21, Jesus shared how a rich man decided to store up even more wealth for himself, but was not rich toward God. *"But God said to him, 'You fool! This very night your life will be demanded from you. Then who will get what you have prepared for yourself?'" (Luke 12:20).*

Perhaps you are under the assumption that you have not sinned and do not need Jesus in your life. You are a really good person. Romans 3:10 states, *"There is no one righteous, not even one."* The apostle Paul writes in Romans 3:23, *"For all have sinned and fall short of the glory of God."* In Romans 6:23 he states, *"For the wages of sin is death, but the gift of God is eternal life in Christ Jesus our Lord."*

Maybe at some point in your life you accepted Jesus Christ as your Savior, but you have drifted away from following Him. You have never made Jesus the Lord of your life. Instead of seeking Him for His will and direction for your life, your attitude has been "it's all about me. I am in charge and you (God) cannot tell me what to do. Maybe one day down the road I will serve You, but not now." You have neglected the most important matters in life and where you will spend eternity. Pride rules your life.

Maybe you are mad at God. Do you feel He has abandoned you or been unfair to you or a family member? Has He "picked on you?" Has your trust in Him wavered? Have you been hurt by Christians and do not want anything to do with Christianity? Have you sinned big time and think God can never forgive you? The blood Jesus shed on the cross brings atonement for us. He is faithful to cleanse us from all unrighteousness and from all of our iniquities. *"But if we walk in the light, as He is in the light, we have fellowship with one another, and the blood of Jesus, His son, purifies us from all sin. If we claim to be without sin, we deceive ourselves and the truth is not in us. If we confess our sins, He is faithful and just and will forgive us our sins and purify us from all unrighteousness. If we claim we have not sinned, we make Him out to be a liar, and His word has no place in our lives" (I John 1:7-10).*

Paul wrote in Romans 10:9-10, *"That if you confess with your mouth 'Jesus is Lord,' and believe in your heart that God raised Him from the dead, you will be saved. For it is with your heart that you believe and are justified, and it is with your mouth that you confess and are saved."*

No matter which scenario you fall into, pray the following prayer to accept Jesus Christ as your Savior and become a born again believer. Make Him the Lord of your life. Do not hold back! *"And everyone who calls on the name of the Lord will be saved" (Acts 2:21).*

Dear Jesus, I am sorry for my sins. I am sorry for hurting You and disobeying You. I repent of my sins. I believe You died on the cross for me and Your blood washes away my sins. I believe You rose from the dead. Come into my heart. Come into my life. Be the Savior and Lord of my life. Take my talents and abilities and use them for your glory. I surrender my life to you. I love You. Amen.

If you prayed this prayer, then I challenge you to tell someone. Also, read your Bible on a daily basis. Begin with the Gospel of John. Get a translation that is easy for you to understand. Find a Bible believing church and begin attending the services regularly. Your journey of faith has begun!